THE GLORIES OF SAINT JOSEPH

Compiled by
The Monks of St. Joseph Abbey

Traditions Monastiques

Cum permissu Superiorum

"Joseph was the guardian, the administrator and the legitimate and natural defender of the divine household of which he was the head. It is thus natural and very worthy of St. Joseph that, as he supported in another era all the needs of the Family of Nazareth which he wrapped in his holy protection, he now covers with his heavenly patronage and defends the Church of Jesus Christ."

(Pope Leo XIII, *Quamquam Pluries*, 1889)

"This patronage must be invoked, and it is always necessary for the Church, not only to defend it against dangers ceaselessly cropping up, but also and above all to support it in those fearful efforts at evangelizing the world, and spreading the new evangelization among nations where the Christian religion and life were formerly the most flourishing, but are now put to a difficult test. . . . May St. Joseph become for all a singular master in the service of the saving mission of Christ that is incumbent on each and every one of us in the Church: To spouses, to parents, to those who live by the work of their hands or by any other work, to persons called to the contemplative life as well as to those called to the apostolate."

(Pope John Paul II, *Redemptoris Custos*, 1989)

TABLE OF CONTENTS

FOREWORD

This little book makes no other claim than to provide food for thought to those who wish to know more about the life and virtues of the chaste Spouse of the Mother of God. In reading these pages, they will form a more precise idea of his action and power, which are always ready to help souls of good will.

The texts are drawn mainly from the works of the saints and doctors of the Church, but also from other authors whose writings have been admitted by the Church. They may prove helpful for meditation.

As for the stories of graces obtained through the intercession of this great saint, we would have liked to present a greater selection, dealing with conversions or other spiritual graces. However, the recipients of such gifts often wish to keep them hidden. The more common accounts reported here are nevertheless of a nature to inspire or increase confidence in St. Joseph, and to encourage the readers to invoke him in situations devoid of human solutions.

These texts are arranged in the guise of a "Month of St. Joseph"—that is to say, a written meditation, an account of graces obtained, a prayer and a short practical resolution, for each day of the month of March, which is especially consecrated by the Church to the honor of this saint (They may also be used for any other month of the year).

The Catechism of the Catholic Church, published by the Holy See in 1992, exhorts us to "prepare ourselves for the hour of our death" by asking for the intercession of the Mother of God and by "entrusting ourselves to St. Joseph, patron of a happy death."[1] It is our wish that the following pages will encourage the reader to lead, in company with St. Joseph, a life that is truly Christian and which corresponds more and more with God's plan for him, in order to merit, by his protection, a death that is peaceful and holy before God.

We thank all those who have been kind enough to help us compile this humble book, especially the Reverend Mother General of the Little Sisters of the Poor.

May St. Joseph continue, from Heaven, to protect and guide the Holy Family which is the Catholic Church.

September 8, 1993
✠ Fr. Augustin-Marie Joly, O.S.B.
Abbot (emeritus) of Saint-Joseph de Clairval

1. No. 1014

PREFACE TO THE ENGLISH VERSION

Since the publication of the first French edition under the title *St. Joseph, Époux de Marie*, this humble work in honor of our glorious patron has been translated into Dutch and German and has gone through two successive French editions, both of which included corrections, additions and substitutions, especially with regard to the stories of graces obtained through his intercession.

This first English edition, while including all the modifications of the third French edition, presents a few novelties vis-à-vis the original. First of all, the prayers or hymns—more numerous than in the French—, instead of being all grouped together at the end, are dispersed throughout the book, with at least one prayer or hymn being assigned to each day of the month, making easier a daily act of devotion in honor of St. Joseph. At the beginning and at the end of the volume are to be found still other prayers, generally longer and adapted to particular persons or circumstances. Special attention must be paid to the Thirty Days' Prayer to St. Joseph in Honor of the Thirty Years Spent with

Jesus and Mary,[1] which may be recited each day of the month instead of or in addition to the shorter prayer given for each day. An index of all the prayers will be found at the end of the volume in order to facilitate the finding of any given prayer.[2] The prayer of St. Francis de Sales to St. Joseph, placed before the resolution for the Seventh Day,[3] is recited daily by our community for all our friends and benefactors. Another important difference with regard to the original is the addition of a few texts, e.g., the account of St. Joseph's death by the Venerable Mary of Agreda,[4] and the poem of St. Joseph addressing the Child Jesus by St. Alphonsus.[5]

Last but not least, we take this opportunity to express our most sincere gratitude to all those generous persons who made this English version possible by giving us freely of their time either by translating part of the text into English, or by proof-reading and correcting a text already translated. Their names are as follows:

Mrs. R. ALFONSO (Canada); Mr. A. BLAKE (Canada); Mrs. C. CASTAGNARO (Canada); Mr. J. CLOUGH (U.K.); Mr. E. COLE (U.S.A.); Rev. Fr. G. CONACHER, O.S.B. (U.K.); Mr. A. DELARUE (U.K.); Rev. Fr. P. DIAMOND (Canada); Mr. R. J.

1. Cf. pp. 13-16
2. Cf. pp. 252-253.
3. Cf. p. 67
4. Cf. Twenty-Eighth Day, pp. 201-203.
5. Cf. Twenty-Third Day, pp. 169-170.

DOLBEC (Canada); Miss. A. FOUNTAINE (U.K.); Mr. M. FULLER (U.S.A.); Ms. A. GENDREAU (Canada); Mr. D. HEINER (U.S.A.); Mrs. S. HERTZ (U.S.A.); Mr. R. KEELER (U.K.); Sr. MARGUERITE (India); Ms. M.-P. MARTIN-MENNENS (U.S.A.); Mr. P. MAURICE (U.S.A.); Mrs. Z. PERSIDSKY (U.S.A.); Mr. W. RAMSAY (Ireland); the late Rev. Fr. D. F. ROCHFORD (U.K.); Mrs. R. SAMPSON (U.K.); Mr and Mrs M. STRUELENS (U.S.A.); THÉRÈSE and JEANNE of the bilingual lay community at Madonna House situated in Paris (France); Mrs. V. UDRYS (U.S.A.); Mr. P. WADDELOVE (U.S.A.); Sr. YVONNE OF THE CHILD JESUS (India); Mrs. C. ZAFFARONI (Canada).

We pray that St. Joseph, Foster-Father of Our Lord Jesus Christ and Spouse of the Immaculate Mother of God will reward them as only he can do. We hope as well that this book, offered to the Blessed Trinity in grateful homage for all that we have received through the intercession of our Holy Patron, may bring light, consolation and strength to all its readers.

GLORIA JESU PER MARIAM ET JOSEPH!

FEASTS OF ST. JOSEPH

Besides dedicating the month of March to St. Joseph, Holy Church shows her supreme love and veneration for her heavenly patron by the annual celebration of two feasts in his honor.

On March 19th she solemnly commemorates the death of St. Joseph, which, according to tradition, occurred on that day. On this feast he is venerated in particular as the Spouse of the Virgin Mary and the Patron of the Universal Church, and his protection is invoked by the faithful in order to obtain the grace of a happy death.

On May 1st of each year is celebrated the feast of St. Joseph the Worker, which was established by Pope Pius XII in 1955 in order to christianize the concept of labor and give to all workmen a model and a protector. By the daily labor in his workshop, offered to God with patience and joy, St. Joseph provided for the necessities of his Holy Spouse and of the Incarnate Son of God, and thus became an example to all laborers. "Workmen and all those laboring in conditions of poverty will have reasons to rejoice rather than to grieve, since they have in common with the Holy Family daily pre-occupations and cares" (Pope Leo XIII).

Pious custom also dedicates Wednesday of each week to the honor of St. Joseph and, in the past, indulgences were granted for any pious exercises performed on the first Wednesday of the month.

Thirty Days' Prayer to St. Joseph In Honor of the Thirty Years Spent with Jesus and Mary

(May be recited daily during the Thirty Days' Devotion)

Ever blessed and glorious Joseph, kind and indulgent father, and compassionate friend of all in sorrow, through that bitter grief with which thy heart was saturated when thou didst behold the sufferings of the Infant Saviour, and in prophetic view didst contemplate His most ignominious passion and death, take pity, I beseech thee, on my poverty and necessity, counsel me in my doubts, and console me in all my anxieties.

Thou art the good father and protector of orphans, the advocate of the defenseless, the patron of those who are in need and desolation. Do not then disregard the petition of thy poor child. My sins have drawn down upon me the just displeasure of my God, and hence I am surrounded with sorrows. To thee, O loving guardian of the poor neglected Family of Nazareth, do I fly for shelter and protection.

Listen, then, I entreat thee, with a father's solicitude, to the earnest prayer of thy poor supplicant, and obtain for me the object of my petition.

I ask it by that infinite mercy of the Eternal Son of God, which induced Him to assume our nature and to be born into this world of sorrow.

I ask it by that humility which filled thy heart when, awed by the mystery wrought in thy Immaculate Spouse, thou didst regard thyself as unworthy of her.

I ask it by that weariness, solicitude, and suffering which thou didst endure when thou soughtest in vain at the inns of Bethlehem a shelter for the Holy Virgin, and a birthplace for the Infant God, and when, being everywhere refused, thou wert obliged to consent that the Queen of Heaven should give birth to the world's Redeemer in a wretched stable.

I ask it by the painful blood-shedding thou didst witness at His Circumcision.

I ask it by the sweetness and power of that sacred Name, Jesus, which thou didst confer on the adorable Infant.

I ask it by that mortal anguish inflicted on thee by the prophecy of Holy Simeon, which declared the Child Jesus and His Holy Mother to be the future victims of our sins and of their own great love for us.

I ask it through that sorrow and anguish which filled thy soul, when the Angel declared to thee that the life of the Child Jesus was sought by His enemies, from whose impious design thou wast obliged to flee with Him and His Blessed Mother into Egypt.

I ask it by all the pains, fatigues and toils of that long and perilous journey.

I ask it by all the sorrows thou didst endure in Egypt, when sometimes thou wast unable, even by the sweat of thy brow, to procure daily food for thy poor Family.

I ask it by all thy solicitude to protect the Sacred Child and His Immaculate Mother during thy second journey, when thou wast ordered to return to thy native country.

I ask it by the peaceful dwelling in Nazareth, in which so many joys and sorrows were mingled.

I ask it by thy extreme affliction in being for three days deprived of the company of the Adorable Child.

I ask it by thy joy at finding Him in the Temple, and by the unspeakable consolation imparted to thee in the cottage of Nazareth, while living in the company of the Infant Jesus.

I ask it by that wonderful condescension by which He subjected Himself to thy will.

I ask it through that sorrowful foresight thou hadst continually in thy mind of all the Infant Jesus was to suffer, when thou shouldst no longer be at His side.

I ask it by that painful contemplation by which thou foresawest those Divine Infant Hands and Feet, now so active in serving thee, one day pierced with cruel nails; that Head which rested gently on thy breast, crowned with sharp thorns; that delicate Body which thou didst tenderly fold in thy mantle and press to thy heart, stripped, mangled, and extended on a cross.

I ask it by that heroic sacrifice of thy will and best affections, by which thou didst offer up to the Eternal Father the last awful moment when the God-Man was to expire for our salvation.

I ask it by that perfect love and conformity with which thou didst receive the divine order to depart from this life, and from the company of Jesus and Mary.

I ask it by that exceeding great joy which filled thy soul, when the Redeemer of the world, triumphant over death and hell, entered into the possession of His kingdom, and conducted thee also into it with especial honors.

I ask it through Mary's glorious Assumption and through that endless bliss, which with her thou wilt eternally derive from the presence of God.

O good Father! I beseech thee, by all thy sufferings, sorrows, and joys, to hear me, and obtain the grant of my earnest petitions. (*Here name them or reflect upon them*). Obtain for all those who have asked my prayers all that is useful to them in the designs of God. And finally, my dear Patron and Father, be thou with me, and all who are dear to me, in our last moments, that we may eternally chant the praise of Jesus, Mary, and Joseph. Amen.

FIRST DAY

Testimony of St. Teresa of Avila

In her *Life*, the great Carmelite saint relates an illness which tested her for three years. This is how she speaks of St. Joseph:

"My extreme weakness cannot be described, for I was nothing but skin and bones. I remained in this condition for more than eight months, and, though my paralysis kept improving, it continued for nearly three years. When I began to get about on my hands and knees, I praised God. . . . Throughout the time I was so ill, I kept a strict watch over my conscience to drive away from me the very shadow of mortal sin. Unfortunate being that I was, I longed for health that I might serve God better!. . . .

"When I found myself, still so young, struck with paralysis, and saw the sorry state to which earthly doctors had reduced me, I decided to have recourse to heavenly ones to obtain my cure. This was the object of my desires—without, however, depriving me of the great joy with which I endured my sickness—even though it occurred to me that, if a return to health was to bring about my damnation, it would be infinitely better for me to remain as I was. Nevertheless, I could not drive away the thought that if I were restored to health I would serve the Lord with a much greater devotion. Alas! it is one of our illusions not to surrender fully to God who knows, better than we, what is good for us.

"To make the Lord grant me my wishes, I asked that Masses be said for me, and I had recourse to highly recommended prayers. I took St. Joseph as my advocate and protector, and recommended myself very earnestly to him. He came to my help in the most visible manner. This loving father of my soul, this beloved protector, hastened to pull me out of the state in which my body was languishing, just as he snatched me away from greater dangers of another nature which were jeopardizing my honor and my eternal salvation! For my happiness to be complete, he has always answered my prayers beyond what I had asked and hoped for.

"I do not remember even now that I have ever asked anything of him which he has failed to grant. I am astonished at the great favors which God has bestowed on me through this blessed saint, and at the perils from which He has freed me, both in body and in soul. To other saints the Lord seems to have given grace to help us in one or other of our necessities, but of this glorious saint my experience is that he succors us in them all, and that the Lord wishes to teach us that as He was Himself subject to him on earth—for, being His guardian and being called His father, he could command Him—in like manner in Heaven He still does all that he asks. This has also been the experience of other persons whom I have advised to commend themselves to him; and even today there are many who have great devotion to him through having newly experienced this truth. I wish I could persuade everyone to be devoted to this glorious saint, for I have long experience of the great blessings which he can obtain from God. I have never known anyone who was truly devoted to him and who rendered him particular services who did not notably advance in virtue, for he gives very real help to souls who commend themselves to him.

"For some years now, I have been asking for a special favor on his feast day, and it has always been granted. If, through some imperfection, my request was in any way moving away from the goal—the glory of God—he would rectify it so that I might draw a greater good from it.

"If I were a person writing with authority, I would gladly describe, at greater length and in the minutest detail, the favors which this glorious saint has granted to me and to others. I only beg, for the love of God, that anyone who does not believe me will put what I say to the test, and he will see by experience what great advantages come from his commending himself to this glorious patriarch and having particular devotion to him. Those who practice prayer should have a childish affection for him always. I do not know how anyone can think of the Queen of the Angels, during the time that she suffered so much with the Child Jesus, without giving thanks to St. Joseph for the perfect way he helped them. Let anyone who cannot find a master to teach him how to pray, take this glorious saint as his master and he will not go astray.

"Finally, his power and goodness shone upon me. Thanks to him I felt my strength return, I arose, I walked: my paralysis was cured!" (*Life,* ch. 6).

In her filial piety, St. Teresa of Avila never failed to call St. Joseph: *Señor y padre mio*: My Lord and my Father.

Do What He Tells You!

St. Teresa of Avila had left Valladolid to found a monastery at Beas, in Andalusia, when, while crossing the Sierra Morena, the wagon drivers lost their way in the passes. Foolishly, they advanced along a path so narrow that they could soon go neither forward nor backward. Teresa and her companions were left hanging over precipices and cliffs, down which they could all fall at the slightest movement.

"My daughters," said the saint, "let us pray to God that, by the intercession of St. Joseph, He may deliver us from this danger."

At that moment, the voice of an old man shouted to them: "Stop! if you go any further, you are doomed!"

"But how can we get out of this terrible situation?" they asked. "Lean your wagon to this side," came the reply, "and turn back."

They followed these directions, and to their great surprise, the guides at once found themselves on an excellent road. Full of gratitude to their deliverer, they ran to thank him to the place from which the voice had spoken. Teresa watched them and, seeing them running at full speed searching in vain, said to her daughters: "Really, I do not know why we let these good men go on running, for what we heard was the voice of my Father St. Joseph, and they will never find him!"

Saved By Alms

A heedless, unbelieving man was about to die with blasphemy on his lips and despair in his heart. His wife was praying and weeping, but God seemed not to hear.

Meanwhile death was fast approaching.

"Go quickly," said the priest to the sick man's wife, "go and look for a pauper and give him alms in the name of St. Joseph for the conversion of your husband."

She ran through the streets, met an old man covered with rags and gave him large alms, telling him to pray for the conversion of a sinner. . . . At that very moment, the dying man had taken the priest's hand, kissed it with tears, and begged forgiveness.

The conversion was sincere and edifying. A few hours later, the man entered into eternity, saved by the alms given in the name of St. Joseph and by the prayer of the pauper.

✠

Litany of St. Joseph

Lord, have mercy
Christ, have mercy
Lord, have mercy
Christ, hear us
Christ, graciously hear us
God, the Father of Heaven, have mercy on us
God the Son, Redeemer of the world, have mercy on us
God the Holy Spirit, have mercy on us
Holy Trinity, one God, have mercy on us

Holy Mary,	pray for us
St. Joseph,	"
Illustrious Son of David,	"
Splendor of Patriarchs,	"
Spouse of the Mother of God,	"

Chaste guardian of the Virgin, ”
Foster-father of the Son of God, ”
Diligent defender of Christ, ”
Head of the Holy Family, ”
Joseph most just, ”
Joseph most pure, ”
Joseph most prudent, ”
Joseph most strong, ”
Joseph most obedient, ”
Joseph most faithful, ”
Mirror of patience, ”
Lover of poverty, ”
Model of workers, ”
Glory of home life, ”
Guardian of virgins, ”
Mainstay of families, ”
Comfort of the afflicted, ”
Hope of the sick, ”
Patron of the dying, ”
Terror of demons, ”
Protector of Holy Church, ”

Lamb of God, who takest away the sins of the world, spare us, O Lord

Lamb of God, who takest away the sins of the world, graciously hear us, O Lord

Lamb of God, who takest away the sins of the world, have mercy on us.

℣. He made him master of His Household.

℟. And the ruler of all His possessions.

Let us pray

O God, in Thy loving providence, Thou didst choose Blessed Joseph to be the Spouse of Thy most Holy Mother; grant us the favor of having him for our intercessor in Heaven whom on earth we venerate as our Protector, Thou, who livest and reignest forever and ever. Amen.

In honor of St. Joseph

Do everything with confidence and trust in St. Joseph, who makes the impossible possible.

SECOND DAY

Day or Night?

It is interesting to ponder over which is more impressive, the day or the night.

The day is magnificent, but the night is so solemn! The day enlightens the earth for us, while the night unveils the sky. These thoughts come to us as we think of St. Joseph.

We are struck by the obscurity which surrounds this incomparable saint.

We know many facts and stories about earthly celebrities, but none about St. Joseph. All we have are a few lines about him in the Gospel, but not a single quote. As far as the world is concerned, his life is as obscure as night itself: deep, majestic, and spiritually moving. So much so that although he is hidden, in the end we find his life greater, more beautiful and far more appealing than the lives of others which are bathed in light.

The spiritual depth hidden behind this shadowy image grows clearer as one fathoms it, and eventually the soul feels itself standing before a great abyss. Without knowing it, the soul is lifted above the ordinary realm of our thoughts into air which is purer, more fragrant, as if a breeze blew gently from our heavenly home. We are at peace, and dwell close to God. The impression we receive when we approach St. Joseph is the same as that which we encounter when entering a shrine. A shrine is peaceful, silent; it has a certain obscurity which recollects our spirit. Its atmosphere is sober, profound, gentle; it inspires respect and it humbles, making one forget the world in a foretaste of Heaven. Whichever shrine it is, it is a house of God. I doubt that one can think of St. Joseph without experiencing some of these feelings. St. Joseph is, in his being, the surrounding and the setting for the greatest of all mysteries: that of God made man in the womb of a Virgin; that of Jesus and Mary.

Liturgical rubrics stipulate that the Holy Eucharist be kept in our tabernacles, in a gold or silver ciborium, and that this be covered with a gold, silver or silk veil. In the mystery of the Incarnation, the Sacred Host is Jesus, the ciborium is Mary, the veil is St. Joseph. Just as the ciborium is only there for the Host, so the veil is only there for the Host and the ciborium. As Mary exists and lives only for Jesus, Joseph exists and lives only for Jesus and Mary (Bishop Gay).

Father John of Fontfroide and the Circus Manager

Toward the end of the nineteenth century, Father John, abbot of Fontfroide, France, witnessed a special favor granted by St. Joseph, to a soul who was in the habit of praying to him. Here is how he relates it:

"During my stay in Sénanque (France), one night, I went for a walk in a courtyard near the main entrance where I didn't usually go. The brother porter came to get me.

'A man is asking for you!'

'Me! He knows me?'

'He must. He saw you, and pointed you out.'

"I went to see him. He was a good-looking man, very well-dressed, with distinguished manners, but he looked troubled. A few steps away from him, a superb black horse was browsing, the most beautiful horse I had ever seen. What a striking animal!

'Sir,' said the visitor, 'I do not know you. I saw you from a distance and sent for you. Save me! I was going to drown myself, but did not succeed. My horse carried me over the rocks and stopped at your door. Where am I? What is this house? A country house?'

'No, a monastery.'

'I have never seen one before. And why are you dressed in black and white like a clown?'

'It is the habit of our Order. But tell me who you are.'

'I am the manager of the Imperial Circus of Lyon.'

'And you went bankrupt?'

'No, Sir. I am well-off and business is excellent! I have many people working for me, but I am haunted by the idea of ending my life.'

"I took him by the arm and said, smiling:

'No, you are not going to drown yourself; the water is too cold! We will look after your horse. Come and tell me your story and we shall see what can be done.'

"This unusual man immediately told the extraordinary story which follows:

'I never knew my father. My mother died when I was seven. It was evening. A procession of people came to get her. Before this, a priest had come accompanied by children who were dressed up in red: headdress, belt and red dress with a kind of lacework over all.

'I was struck by this. Later, I was told that they had come so she could make her First Communion!

'When she died, I took what was left of her money and went to a nearby circus. I was alone, with no one to turn to. I asked the director of the circus if he would hire me.

"You are too young, tell your father. . . ."

"I have no father."

"Your mother. . . ."

"She was buried today."

"Where do you live?"

'I told him.

"Come back tomorrow, and we shall see. . . ."

'I came back and was hired as a member of his circus. He always treated me as his own son, and when he died I inherited the circus. I travelled all over and made a lot of money. But for some time now, I don't understand what is the matter with me. I am unhappy and I want to drown myself!'

'Do you have the faith?'

'What do you mean?'

'Do you believe in God?'

'Yes, vaguely, but I don't know anything about Him.'

'Do you know how to make the sign of the cross?'

'Mother used to make it and she made me do it, too. I haven't done it since then. She also taught me a prayer which she made me say every day. I will recite it for you.' He then said the prayer: *Ave Joseph*.

'Do you recite this prayer sometimes?'

'I have always prayed it before going to bed.'

'Do you know who St. Joseph is?'

'No.'

'Why are you so unhappy?'

'I really don't know. I have become bored, tired of everything, even of life itself. I urged my horse to the bank of the Rhone, but he sprung back and fled away. This is the first time in my life that I could not control him.'

'Well! It is clearly Providence which brought you here!'

'What is Providence?'

'It is the hand of God made manifest. This is what led you here, because God wants to save you. You have been baptized, and He does not want you to die as a pagan. The Rhone is not what you need; it is in the waters of grace that you must drown yourself. We shall work at it together. Normally, I never come to the garden at this time of night. By inspiring me to come, the good Master sent me to you. With all my heart I pity you; allow me to embrace you.'

"I did so with warmth, and he was touched.

'You will have supper with us, tonight,' I added. 'You can stay overnight. Tomorrow, instead of leaving, you will spend the day here.'

"He stayed in the monastery, not only the next day but for three whole days. I taught him the basic truths. He proved to be very intelligent, and God had already shown him that neither earthly pleasures nor money bring happiness. He went to Confession and Communion. I sent him away against his will. He went back to Avignon a new man, settled his affairs, sold the circus, gave the money to the poor and entered religious life. A few years later, he came down with a high fever and died a very holy death, young and unknown.

"You see," added the good Father, "how valuable it is for a soul to have the protection of St. Joseph. This man was faithful to prayer even without understanding what he was saying, or knowing to whom he was praying. For this he was rewarded."

+

Ave Joseph

Ave, Joseph, gratia Dei abundantius prædite, cuius ulnæ Salvatorem parvulum portaverunt et oculi crescentem aspexerunt: benedictus es inter viros, et benedictus filius almæ Sponsæ tuæ, Jesus.

Sancte Joseph, qui unigenito Dei in patrem es electus, quamdiu in terris inter familiæ, valetudinis, laborisque curas versamur, ora pro nobis et, morte imminente, nobis subvenire dignare. Amen.

Hail, Joseph, filled with divine grace, in whose arms the Saviour was carried and under whose eyes He grew up: blessed art thou among men and blessed is Jesus, the Son of thy dear Spouse.

Holy Joseph, chosen to be a father to the Son of God, pray for us in the midst of our cares of family, health and work, and deign to assist us at the hour of our death. Amen.[1]

In honor of St. Joseph

Strive to love silence and the hidden life as St. Joseph did, without seeking to be noticed by others.

1. Cf. another version of this prayer on Twenty-Second Day, p. 165.

THIRD DAY

The Desire to Please Our Lady

We know very little about the life of St. Joseph. An ancient writer even remarked that, although three or four of his deeds are mentioned in the Gospels, we do not find even one of his words. Perhaps it is because the evangelists were so totally preoccupied, or even overwhelmed, with the marvels they had to communicate about the Saviour of the world, that their attention could not be extended further. Perhaps it is because the Holy Spirit intended this silence to highlight in some way the principal characteristics of St. Joseph: his humility, his love for solitude and the hidden life. Nevertheless, this very light sketch hardly covers what we would have liked to know about the life of this exceptional saint. What touching examples are lost forever! What excellent maxims are buried and forgotten for all time! But the ones most likely to deplore this lack of information are those who are married. It seems to me that their regrets must be all for themselves, rather than for St. Joseph. Even if the Holy Gospels have only quoted two words about him, *Virum Mariæ*, meaning that he was the husband of Mary, this is sufficient to give us the most laudable idea of his saintliness. It is enough to inspire the eloquence of the Christian orators.

Far from complaining about a lack of information on my subject, I have to say that these two words seem to me to enfold such a world of meaning that I find myself overwhelmed both by the number and by the grandeur of the things which they imply. If I could adequately express all that I mean by this, I have no doubt that I would render due honor to this incomparable spouse, but because I know that cannot possibly fully satisfy you, what else can I do but turn to the Blessed Virgin? I know that she would want us to honor this saint so dear to her through the most sacred bonds; I hope she will obtain insights for you to make up for the inadequacy of my words and thoughts.

Even if there were no other reason to praise St. Joseph, we should do so in order to please Mary. There is no doubt that she strongly supports every effort to revere this saint; she herself would be honored by this. Besides the fact that he was her true husband and she always felt for him all that a virtuous wife should feel for the man to whom the Lord had bound her so closely, what gratitude must she not have felt towards him for the way he exercised his authority and for the way he respected her virginal purity! Her gratitude was equal to the love which she herself had for this virtue, and therefore, nothing could be more lively than her zeal for the honor of St. Joseph (St. Claude de la Colombière).

Holy Death in a Wicked House

During the night of January 2, 1885, an old man presented himself to a priest asking him to come to the bedside of a dying woman and indicating the address to which he wanted to take him.

The street that the old man pointed out was one of ill repute. The old man himself was a total stranger, and night was falling. The priest feared that it might be a trap, so he hesitated; but the old man urged him on.

"We cannot delay; it involves giving the Last Rites to a poor old woman at the point of death."

Faced with such a sacred duty, the priest no longer hesitated and followed the messenger. The night was bitterly cold, but the old man did not seem to notice. He went ahead and said to the priest:

"I will wait for you at the door."

The door in front of which they stopped belonged to one of the most notorious houses of the area, and the priest, who was carrying the Blessed Sacrament, had another moment of apprehension. But remembering that Our Lord came to save sinners, on the instruction of his guide, he pulled hard on the bell. There was no reply.

He knocked several times, but there was still no response.

The old man was standing back at a distance, and the priest finally said to him:

"As you can see, this is hopeless. No one is coming to let us in. . . ."

"Let me knock," replied the mysterious person, stepping forward as the priest drew back. "As soon as the door is opened, go in quickly. Go up the stairs and open the door of the bedroom at the end of the hall; there you will find the dying woman."

These strange words were spoken with such authority that the priest made no objection. The old man knocked on the door in a peculiar way, and it opened immediately. This time the priest did not hesitate; he entered, climbed the stairs, opened the door that had been indicated, and found a woman stretched out on a bed of pain, who, between her cries of agony, constantly repeated:

"A priest! A priest! They are going to let me die without a priest."

The minister of God approached her:

"My daughter, a priest is here."

But she did not believe him.

"No," she cried out. "No one in this house would care to fetch a priest."

"My daughter, an old man brought me to you."

" I don't know any old man," replied the dying woman.

Nevertheless, the priest managed, little by little, to convince her that he was indeed the minister of God for whom she had been calling, and he offered her the sacraments.

She confessed to a long life of sin which had been weighing heavily on her conscience. She showed such lively contrition that the priest, astonished at meeting such faith in a person so completely separated from God, asked her if she had not kept up some devotional practice.

"None," she said, "except a prayer that I used to recite each day to St. Joseph, to obtain a happy death."

The priest prepared everything for the Last Rites and, during this time, several people entered the bedroom, then left without appearing to notice him.

He gave the repentant sinner Holy Communion as well as Extreme Unction and left her only when, very peacefully, she gave up her purified soul into the hands of Jesus Christ.

The priest was alone and did not meet anyone as he left the house and returned home.

While thinking about the events of that night and of his consoling mission, he became firmly convinced that the charitable old man was none other than the glorious and merciful St. Joseph, patron saint of a happy death.

✠

Prayer for a Happy Death

O Blessed Joseph, who didst yield thy last breath in the fond embrace of Jesus and Mary, when the seal of death shall close my career in life, come, holy Father, with Jesus and Mary, to aid me, and obtain for me this only solace which I ask for in that hour, to die encircled by their holy arms. Into your sacred hands, living and dying, Jesus, Mary, Joseph, I commend my soul. Amen.

In honor of St. Joseph

Ardently spread the devotion to St. Joseph in the belief that this observance is very dear to the Immaculate Heart of Mary.

FOURTH DAY

Prepared by Grace

God, who is the supremely perfect Being, is also for His creatures the source of all good. Inasmuch as He is infinitely wise, however, He distributes His benefits according to the rule which He Himself laid down from all eternity in His supreme counsels. That clear vision of worldly events, together with the will to fulfill them in time, is what we call Providence; but in the case of a reasonable creature, endowed with free will and destined by God to enjoy Him in Heaven, it is called predestination.

In theological language, predestination, the expression of God's infinite charity towards angels and men, is defined as *the preexistence in God of the order or plan regulating the transmission of reasonable creatures to that special end which is eternal life.*[1] In its formal concept, predestination presupposes not

1. St. Thomas Aquinas, *Summa Theologica*, 1a pars, q. 23, a. 1, corpus.

only the heavenly glory which is its end, but also everything which might be conducive to it in an individual's life.

Thus, inasmuch as St. Joseph's election to the dignity of Spouse of Mary and foster-father of Jesus would constitute the formal reason of his future glory, it follows that he was predestined to this dignity from all eternity, even as Jesus Christ Himself was predestined to be the Son of God and Mary to be the Mother of the Word Incarnate. St. Joseph will therefore occupy a preeminent place among the elect next to the Virgin Mother, and this place no one will take from him, for what is established in the divine counsels cannot be frustrated. The order of predestination suffers no change.

St. Joseph's predestination to the dignity of Spouse of the Mother of God was entirely subordinated to the decree of the Incarnation of the Word, not fortuitously, but precisely in view of the fact that the Incarnation was ordained to the salvation of mankind.

In point of fact, according to the teaching of St. Thomas, which agrees admirably with Sacred Scripture and the liturgy, if man had not sinned, the Word would not have become incarnate. That is why the predestination of St. Joseph, like Christ's and His Mother's, had the redemption of the human race as its formal object.

Here, therefore, appears in all its beauty the radiant crown which was destined from all eternity to wreathe the head of the glorious patriarch.

Inasmuch as the Redemption was to be accomplished only by the sacrifice of Jesus Christ on the Cross, St. Joseph was predestined first of all to be the authentic witness of the Saviour's supernatural birth and then to become the guardian of the Virgin Mother and her Son, watching over them with unswerving fidelity and providing their food and necessities by the work of his hands.

That is why it can be said that St. Joseph was predestined by God to cooperate in a special manner with the Saviour and His Mother in the work of Redemption; and there precisely lies the sublimity of the office which so enhances the holy patriarch's dignity in our eyes.

We rejoice, O glorious Patriarch, in the choice which the Most High made of you for so sublime a dignity. For, sinners that we are, we dare have confident recourse to you, in light of the fact that our very faults somehow supplied the motive for your predestination, inasmuch as you were chosen to be "the minister of our salvation."[1] Be our guide to Jesus, Prince of the predestined, and intercede for us with her who holds the key to all graces and whom in all truth you call your well-beloved Spouse (Cardinal Lepicier).

1. Hymn *Cælitum, Joseph,* for the feasts of St. Joseph, p. 87.

"Don't Take This Plane!"

A Jewish lawyer, who was a Catholic convert, was arrested by the Nazis in 1939 and deported to Buchenwald camp. Three weeks later he was released on condition that he leave the country, abandoning his wife Gertrude and his ten year old daughter, Irene.

After his departure, the Nazis importuned his young wife, who was not Jewish, and proposed to her that she become a "mother of honor" of the Grand Reich. She refused the offer saying that she wished to remain faithful to her husband. Threatened with reprisals, her situation became critical. Full of confidence she turned to Mary and decided to flee. Although she had no official papers, she booked seats for herself and her daughter on a flight for September 1, 1939.

Shortly afterwards, in the middle of the night, she was awakened by a voice. She heard her name distinctly: "Gertrude, don't take this plane, take the one before it!" She was wondering if she had been dreaming. Just as she was about to fall asleep again, she heard the same voice insisting: "Do not take this plane, but the one which leaves before it."

In the morning she followed this advice. Alas! All the seats were booked on the plane in question. Disappointed, Gertrude returned home. As she arrived, the phone rang: "Two people have cancelled their flight. If you are still interested. . . ."—"Yes, most certainly," replied Gertrude.

There she was with her daughter, in the plane, without official papers. She was worried. A gentleman, sitting across from her, remarked: "You look sad. Can I help you in any way?" Gertrude confided her troubles to him. "Very well," replied the stranger; "in that case, you and your daughter will be my guests!"

Upon landing, the gentleman made his way to the exit, accompanied by Gertrude and her daughter. While the other passengers were closely checked by customs officials and the police, our three travellers passed unnoticed and arrived in the large waiting hall.

When Gertrude turned to thank the kind traveller, she discovered he had disappeared in the crowd. She looked for him in vain. Could it be that the Mother of God had sent her spouse St. Joseph to help the two fugitives, he who had known flight and exile? One is led to believe that is what happened.

The second miracle! The following day, they learned that the plane scheduled for September 1 had not been able to take off, because of the onset of the war.

Afterwards, Mary and Joseph helped Gertrude to find her husband again. All three found refuge in a convent of a religious order and, at the end of the war, they were able to return to Germany, safe and sound.

St. Joseph's Censorship

Here is an interesting letter addressed to the superior of a religious community, dated February 17, 1991. May it increase our own esteem for St. Joseph.

"Dear Reverend Father,

"Would you be so kind as to celebrate a Mass of thanksgiving in honor of St. Joseph?

"It is because of him that my eldest son, John, was able to keep his job which was threatened by powerful adversaries. John was in charge of book sales in a large store and, as he refused to sell any obscene or occult books or any other reprehensible literature, they gave him a choice: no 'censorship' or no job. So we prayed to St. Joseph. O, how much!

"The result was that, the next day, the people in question offered their sincere apologies to John and asked him to stay on at his job. It is quite simply miraculous when one considers the hopelessness of the situation.

"Yours faithfully, etc."

+

Prayer to St. Joseph to Obtain a Special Favor

O Blessed St. Joseph, tender-hearted father, faithful guardian of Jesus, chaste Spouse of the Mother of God, I pray thee to join with me in praising God the Father through His Divine Son who died on the cross and rose again to give us sinners new life. Through the holy Name of Jesus, pray with me that we may obtain from the Eternal Father the favor we ask for. . . .

We have been unfaithful to the unfailing love of God the Father; beg of Jesus mercy for us His brethren. Amid the splendors of God's loving presence, do not forget the sorrows of those who suffer, those who pray, those who weep. By thy prayers and those of thy most holy Spouse, our Blessed Lady, may the love of Jesus answer our call of confident hope. Amen.

In honor of St. Joseph

Acquire the habit of consulting God before starting each important action. "Lord, is this action in line with Thy will?"

FIFTH DAY

The Grandeur of St. Joseph

Mary belongs to God; she is the golden ladder by which God wishes to come down to men and to draw them to Himself. But consider this extraordinary fact. Although the Virgin is the beloved one God took for Himself and the wedding chamber in whom the Son chose to unite Himself to His humanity, the Lord saw fit that she should become the spouse of a man, that man being St. Joseph.

Was it in God's plan to give a mortal man some kind of lawful rights over this blessed creature, this holy Virgin? It was indeed—and we are dumbfounded by this act of divine will.

Who, then, is this Joseph, this one chosen by Heaven, this most favored among all men, the one to whom God was pleased to entrust the woman He created with such great love and jealously made His very own? He is a son of David, a close relative of the Virgin. Mary, full of grace though she was, had to live on earth and needed an earthly support, a human arm of flesh and blood to shield and uphold her. Joseph will protect and defend her as his own, for she will be his true spouse.

Such was this son of David's purity of heart that Mary, while she was totally his, could still belong totally to God. They were united in a true marriage, so that each might be closer to God, with, one might say, the help of the other. Concupiscence was extinguished in Joseph, and his soul shone with brilliant purity when he came into the presence of the Blessed Virgin. It could not be that she should be loved by someone who was not perfectly chaste.

We see in St. Joseph a totally purified soul, a soul in which sin has lost its power. St. Augustine, while asserting that no one is ever free from sin in this life and that even the saints must pray "Forgive us our sins," recognized that God could, if He so desired, by way of exception and special privilege, "completely take away the corruption which causes a man to sin and array him with incorruptibility in this life so that he might see God everywhere present, just as the saints in Heaven see Him but without a veil."[1] Surely this marvelous privilege was granted to St. Joseph who was called to virginity in marriage and who had the Son of God always before his eyes. Was he not, as St. Augustine says, completely taken up with unceasing contemplation

1. *De Spiritu et Litt.*, 36, 66. St. Augustine's idea that unceasing contemplation, similar to that of those in Heaven, brings detachment from sin is striking and rich in precious consequences.

of his God? How could he sin? In the holy house of Nazareth, there was no place for sin.

O Joseph, we catch a glimpse of your holiness in its dazzling mystery—Mary can be yours, but no less God's for all that. Furthermore, being yours, she belongs to God even more than before, and it is when she became yours that the great mystery for which she was created was accomplished in her.

How admirable God's arrangement! How it brought to light St. Joseph's extraordinary purity of soul, he who did not keep the love of the creature for himself but returned everything to God!

What a lesson you teach us, O great Saint! You wanted nothing which is not of God and for God. In Mary, you experienced only God, as Mary experienced only God in you. Obtain for us, great Saint, the grace to be able to imitate such purity of heart (Dom Bernard Maréchaux).

Understanding the Warnings of St. Joseph

In the nineteenth century, a priest employed for several years in pastoral work in France was in frequent contact with the superior of a large women's reformatory run by nuns. This establishment, situated in the country and supported by the generosity of some noble ladies, held at the time more than eight hundred repentant young women who had taken refuge there to escape from vice and shame, and who, apart from the voluntary contributions of kind people, had no other resources than the work of their hands. The superior received orders from several large Parisian stores, and that was what enabled her to support so many people. “Among our eight hundred inmates,” she told the priest, “there are at least four hundred who live like true saints.”

One day, the stores which supplied work to the establishment stopped their orders temporarily. The sisters looked in vain for another outlet. Almost all their resources were gone, and they would soon be unable to continue. “If help does not come,” confided the superior to the priest, “we must resign ourselves either to starve to death or to send our poor girls away. If I send them away, will they not return to vice and be lost forever? I beg you, what am I to do?”—“Turn to St. Joseph,” answered the priest. “Start a novena in his honor with the whole community.”

The superior followed the priest’s advice. Now, at this very time, one of his fellow priests had to go to a provincial town where he was invited to give a sermon on a big feast day. His friend had spoken to him about the poor community’s distress and the novena they had begun to St. Joseph asking for help. On arriving at the city where he was to preach, our missionary went to the hotel. The following morning at five o’clock he heard a knock at his door and opened it. Before him stood a liveried servant who asked him to come and see his mistress, Countess N., who wished very much to speak with him. Despite his surprise, the missionary followed the servant without a moment's hesitation. He found the lady who had summoned him in a state of great agitation.

"Allow me to tell you, Father," she said, "what happened to me last night, and to ask your advice. There appeared before me a venerable old man who ordered me very threateningly to come to the assistance of a certain convent. Since that moment, I can no longer rest, and I am extremely agitated. Tell me, Father, what am I to think of this?"

The priest smiled, knowing perfectly well what it was all about, since his confrere had told him about the novena started in honor of St. Joseph.

"What, are you laughing?" said the lady, "when I am quite beside myself and don't know what to think of all this!"

"I am smiling, Madame," answered the priest, "because I already know the whole story and can give you very good advice."

He told her what he had learned from his confrere concerning the distress of the reformatory and the young women's petition to St. Joseph.

"Don't you think," concluded the priest, "that St. Joseph heard the poor girls' prayer and that he decided to choose you, Madame, as the instrument of his mercy? You are to be pitied if you refuse to understand the warnings of the saint."

After explaining everything to the lady, the missionary took leave of her and returned to his hotel. Again he heard a knock at the door and opened it. There stood the same liveried servant, who gave him a sealed envelope saying that his mistress the countess was sending him the contents. The Father opened the envelope and found inside fifteen thousand francs ($3,000). It was St. Joseph's answer to the invocation of his name.

+

Praises of St. Joseph

(composed by St. John Eudes)

Hail, Joseph, image of God the Father,
Hail, Joseph, father of God the Son,
Hail, Joseph, temple of the Holy Spirit,
Hail, Joseph, beloved of the Most Holy Trinity,
Hail, Joseph, most faithful coadjutor of the great counsel,
Hail, Joseph, most worthy Spouse of the Virgin Mary,
Hail, Joseph, father of all the faithful,
Hail, Joseph, guardian of all those who have embraced holy virginity,
Hail, Joseph, faithful observer of holy silence,
Hail, Joseph, lover of holy poverty,
Hail, Joseph, model of meekness and patience,
Hail, Joseph, mirror of humility and obedience;
Blessed art thou above all men,
Blessed thine eyes, which have seen the things which thou hast seen,

Blessed thine ears, which have heard the things which thou hast heard,
Blessed thy hands, which have touched and handled the Incarnate Word,
Blessed thine arms, which have borne Him who bears all things,
Blessed thy bosom, on which the Son of God fondly rested,
Blessed thy heart, inflamed with burning love,
Blessed be the Eternal Father, Who chose thee,
Blessed be the Son, Who loved thee,
Blessed be the Holy Spirit, Who sanctified thee,
Blessed be Mary, thy spouse, who cherished thee as her spouse and brother,
Blessed be the Angel who served thee as a guardian,
And blessed forever be all who love and bless thee. Amen.

In honor of St. Joseph

Imitate this holy patriarch's vigilance in fulfilling God's will, by keeping one's conscience free from all sin through frequent reception of the Sacrament of Penance.

SIXTH DAY

The Great Dignity of St. Joseph

There is a prophetic figure who embodies the greatness of our saint: according to St. Bernard, Joseph, son of Jacob the patriarch, represents in the distant past the awe-inspiring prerogatives of Mary's spouse.

You will remember the extraordinary dream in which the first Joseph saw the sun and the moon and eleven stars bowing down at his feet.[1] This dream was not one of those which a restless imagination conjures up during sleep; rather, it was an ecstatic vision sent to Joseph by God Himself, not only to show the imminent rise in rank of this sleeping youth, but also to point out the future greatness of our saint.

I leave it to you to ponder over the unbelievable destiny of the first Joseph who saw not only his

1. Cf. *Gen* 37:9.

father, his mother and his brothers, but all of Egypt, prostrate at his feet. I will use this example to illustrate the great dignity of the second Joseph.

Almighty God, who could ever begin to fathom it! Do you not think Joseph was moved to see Jesus and Mary at his feet, as if they were servants, showing the most loving signs of respect? This is what makes me bold enough to assert that Joseph, in order to become Mary's spouse, must have been the greatest person ever to have lived, after the Virgin herself. I don't mean that kind of greatness in which the ambitious boast of their honors to gain the empty respect of men. If you study his lineage you will see that Joseph, not lacking such greatness, could boast of having fourteen kings as ancestors, and as many patriarchs and leaders—none of them as great as he despite their sceptres and crowns. According to St. Bernardine of Siena, Joseph came from a line of such illustrious nobility, reaching nearly to the Heavens and including many prophets and patriarchs, that he was able to bestow earthly nobility on the Word Itself.

However it is not because of this greatness that Joseph is praised. If he has dignity in himself, it is not because of the greatness of his ancestors. His identity as carpenter was as dear to him as the title of prince. The royal sceptre was not more important to him than the workman's hammer. His greatness comes above all from his glorious title: "the just one." This is what pleases him most; for this he will be admired for all time. All Joseph's glories are summed up in the eulogy: Joseph was *a just man.*[2]

If you really want to understand Joseph's greatness as "just": analyse the word itself. It sums up all the virtues and the height of Christian perfection. The holy Father of the Church, St. Maximinus of Turin, tells us the same thing: "Do you wish to know why Joseph is called just? Because he possessed perfectly all the virtues." What more can one say about a man than to say that he possesses all the virtues to a perfect degree? Is this not the highest praise? And who could compare himself in grandeur to Joseph who deserved this praise? Could Adam who, before the fall, appeared with all animals subject to him? Could Moses who commanded creatures with his rod? Could Abraham surrounded by his descendants like a sun in the midst of stars? Call to mind Josue stopping the sun at the command of his voice; Solomon seeing queens prostrate before his throne; and you, miracle workers, show us how nature obeys your commands. Realize, however, that all these powers cannot make you equal to St. Joseph. For you received these powers and virtues only in part, while Joseph had them all and to a perfect degree. Humble yourselves then at his feet, all you prophets, patriarchs, apostles, martyrs, miracle workers, all you great ones of Heaven and earth, just as in ancient times the sun and the moon and the stars bowed down to honor the first Joseph (St. Leonard of Port-Maurice).

---

2. *Mt* 1:19.

How St. Joseph Teaches Latin

A young man aspiring to the priesthood, was residing in the home of the village pastor. He had a great desire to dedicate his life to the service of God and the salvation of souls. Unfortunately, he found Latin so difficult that his generous teacher lost patience and, for a moment, despaired of his success. Despite the efforts, piety and tears of the student, his ordeal continued. "My dear child," said the priest, "I see but one way out of this situation, and it is to place you under the protection of St. Joseph and pray to him fervently to grant you what you are lacking in to pursue your studies; otherwise, we are bound to failure. So, be courageous, and let us pray together, as I have a true confidence that our request shall be granted since all is promised to perseverance in prayer."

The student agreed and placed all his confidence in St. Joseph, praying so fervently that the good patriarch kept him in his care in a marvelous way. The student's mind then grew little by little so that he finished his studies with success. On entering the major seminary, he distinguished himself by his knowledge as much as by his virtue, and was ordained priest with honor. Successively made professor of dogmatic and moral theology, superior and finally vicar general, he was for many years the light and adviser of most of the priests who were under his authority. Of this man of God, what was most noticeable was his full confidence in, and recognition of, his generous benefactor, St. Joseph.

Let us learn from this how powerful on the Heart of Jesus is the humble and persevering prayer addressed to Him through the intercession of the Husband of the Virgin Mary.

Unemployment Inevitable

Many witnesses in recent times prove that St. Joseph still knows how to bring comfort to the afflicted, by intervening on their behalf. Here is an example.

"March 15, 1992

"Dear Friends,

"Please accept this letter of thanks to my beloved patron, St. Joseph; it is long overdue.

"About a year ago, a close friend gave me a book on the life of St. Joseph which had a great effect on me. Due to budget restrictions, my job was to be terminated within a year, and I was really in need of financial assistance at the time. During this period, although unemployment seemed inevitable, I continued to ask St. Joseph for help.

"Recently, a few weeks before the end of my contract, someone approached me with a wonderful job offer, perfectly suited to my professional background and which, moreover, included a substantial raise in salary. Not only did this proposal offer me an excellent job, but equally good possibilities for the future. Truly, I attribute this grace to the powerful intercession of St. Joseph.

"May all those who read this testimony be filled with faith in this powerful saint and be thus inspired to call upon him in time of need."

+

Hymn of Supplication

Hail, Joseph, pious guardian,
Husband of the Virgin Mary,
Educator without equal.

May salvation be granted through thy prayer,
May the fault of the sinful soul
Be pardoned.

May we be liberated through thee,
From all the pain merited
By so many guilty crimes.

May all the grace we implore
Be obtained through thee,
Above all the salvation of the soul.

May thy prayer bring together one day
Our souls with the blessed spirits
In the eternal homeland.

May all troubled souls
Be delivered through thy prayer
From all of their anguish.

May thy intercession with Christ
Procure peace for the universe,
And health for the sick.

Joseph, great son of King David,
O! Think on judgment day,
Of those who believe in Christ.

Intercede with the only Saviour of mankind
That He may deliver us
At the hour of our death.

Protect us in this life
And bring joy to the departed
In the Heaven of the blessed. Amen.

In honor of St. Joseph

Never forget to pray to St. Joseph, our powerful guardian, at least once a day.

SEVENTH DAY

St. Joseph, Our Model in Time of Trial

Although the just are all just, nevertheless there is a great disparity between the particular deeds of their justice.[1]

Some saints excelled in one virtue, some in another. They are all saved, but in different ways, there being as many different sainthoods as there are saints.

O, what a great saint is the glorious St. Joseph! He is not only a patriarch, but the prince of all Patriarchs; he is not simply a Confessor,[2] but still more, for his life contained the generosity of the martyrs and of all the other saints.

Among the virtues which were found to an eminent degree in St. Joseph are courage, perseverance, constancy and strength. Now there is

1. The words "just" and "justice" are often taken in Holy Scripture for "saint" and "saintliness."

2. By the word "confessor" is here meant someone who bears witness to the faith and even to a heroic degree.

a great difference between constancy and perseverance, between strength and courage.

We call constant or steadfast the man who holds firm during the fight, ready to suffer the enemy's attacks without dismay or loss of heart; perseverance is mainly concerned with a kind of inner weariness which comes when our troubles are long-drawn-out and which is one of the most dangerous enemies we meet. Thus, perseverance allows a man to scorn that enemy in such a way that he triumphs by his unbroken conformity and submission to God's will.

Strength enables a man effectively to resist his enemy's attacks; courage is the virtue which not only keeps him ready for battle or resistance in due time, but also encourages him to attack first, when the enemy is off guard.

Thus our glorious St. Joseph was blessed with all these virtues and he practiced them wondrously well. As regards his constancy, how greatly it shone forth, did it not, when he saw Our Lady with child without understanding how such a thing could happen? My God, what distress, what trouble and what grief he endured! Nevertheless, he did not complain once; he was not harsh nor unkind toward his wife; he did not mistreat her for it, remaining just as gentle and respectful as before. But to what courage and strength does not the victory bear witness which he won over the two greatest enemies of man, the devil and the world, by that perfect humility which, as we have seen, he practiced throughout his life. As for perseverance, the contrary of lassitude, that inner enemy which invades us in the long succession of miseries, humiliations, hardships and misfortunes, or simply the various happenings of our lives, how greatly was this saint tested by God and by men, too! (St. Francis de Sales)

A Danish Surgeon and St. Joseph's Face

"A famous Danish surgeon finished his morning prayers with this invocation: 'St. Joseph, pray for us.' Noticing my surprised look, he said to me, smiling, 'We always need that great wonder-worker.'

"That evening, I asked my host to tell me about the times when St. Joseph had intervened in his life. After a moment's hesitation, he said, 'I don't like to speak about my own experiences, especially in matters of religion, but it is perhaps possible for you to make known to others that St. Joseph always helps those who put their whole trust in him.

'Listen, then, to something that I saw with my own eyes and can swear to under oath, as can, too, a criminal who is atoning for his heinous crimes in prison, having been touched by the grace of God.

'One winter night, I took the train from Th. to V. I was alone in the dimly lit compartment with a large sum of money which was to be used to build a new clinic. I must have fallen asleep, or at least dozed off, due to the fatigue caused by my night travels and the urgent operations I had performed. I woke up when a silent shadow bent over me and someone seized my throat. It was impossible to reach the alarm, and I could not break free or call for help. There was a giant trying to force a gag into my mouth!

'I thought of St. Joseph. He had always come to my aid when I called upon him. What would happen now? At that moment a fist from outside the window of the train struck my assailant a tremendous blow. He let go. Our eyes turned simultaneously toward the glass where there appeared a face. . . . this face!'—and the doctor pointed to the statue of St. Joseph on his desk. 'The man who was crushing me with his knee cried out and vanished. As though waking from a dream, I looked around me. The compartment was empty.'

"He opened the drawer of his desk and went on: 'Only this gag and this razor were beside me on the seat. I had made up my mind not to say a word, but it happened that not long afterwards the man surrendered himself to the prison authorities in order to atone for his crimes. He is now serving his sentence with true Christian contrition.

'Tell me, don't we have good reason to honor St. Joseph who has intervened in so many difficult situations? Tell those who are in trouble to put their trust in St. Joseph. He will find a solution to the most desperate cases.' "

+

Prayer of St. Francis de Sales to St. Joseph

Glorious St. Joseph, Spouse of Mary, grant us, we beseech thee, thy paternal protection, through the Heart of Jesus Christ.

O Thou whose infinite power reaches out to all our needs, rendering possible for us that which is impossible, look upon the concerns of thy children with thy fatherly countenance.

In the troubles and sorrows that afflict us, we have confident recourse to thee.

Deign to take under thy loving protection this important and difficult endeavor, the cause of our worries, and dispose its success to the glory of God and to the benefit of His faithful servants. Amen.

In honor of St. Joseph

Resolve to be courageous in adversity as well as in the struggle against self, especially with regard to anger. Never speak or act while angry.

EIGHTH DAY

The Mysteries of St. Joseph

The mysteries of St. Joseph emerge from the Holy Infancy and rise like a cloud of incense. He belongs entirely to that period; except for this, we know nothing about him. It seems that this is the only purpose for which God created him and adorned him with such wonderful holiness, the only task assigned to him. He remains apart from the Passion altogether, nor does it cast upon him the shadows which it spreads in advance over the Mother of Sorrows. Indeed, even before Jesus had left the holy house in Nazareth to begin His public ministry, Joseph had gone to meet his ancestors. Consumed by the flame of divine love, he died in a sweet ecstasy leaning on Jesus' bosom with Mary at his side and, in short, in the presence of all that was most beautiful, most holy, most heavenly on the face of the earth. His childhood is lost in obscurity. But who can doubt that all was disposed so as to be a fitting preparation for the high honor which God was to confer on him? Who can doubt that it was designed to give him the formation and consecration that befitted the foster-father of the Word made flesh? Since he belongs solely to the Holy Infancy, it is not surprising to find that the spirit of devotion towards St. Joseph is the same as the spirit of devotion towards the Child Jesus, but in circumstances which make it still more touching.

In the first place, it is through Joseph that we are present in the stable in Bethlehem, during the sojourn in Egypt and in the house of Nazareth. All that intimate familiarity to which the Infant Saviour deigns to give us a right by His Incarnation, all those small services which He condescends to receive from our love and devotion, all the joy and serenity that fill our hearts at the sight of His infant weakness, finally, all the adoration mingled with fear that the presence of His divinity imposes on us, all of these things Joseph is there to receive or to render, to feel or to show, as it were, in our name. He is there as the representative of all the generations of faithful to come, especially those whose hearts are drawn with a special attraction towards the first mysteries of Jesus.

St. Joseph is in Bethlehem, in Egypt, in the desert and in Nazareth like the shadow of the Eternal Father. It is this which constitutes his sublime dignity. The incommunicable and forever blessed Paternity of God is transmitted to him in a figurative way. He is the foster-father of Jesus: in the eyes of the world he is His true father. He exercises the authority of a father and fulfills the paternal duties of affection and care. Indeed, in His human nature, Our Lord is submitted to St.

Joseph, He who, in His divine nature, is not inferior to the Father. The ineffable treasures of God—Jesus and Mary—are entrusted to the care of St. Joseph; he is both a treasure himself and the guardian of the treasures of God. He has a special part in the plan of Redemption. Like Jesus and Mary, he, too, has his prototypes, his precursors and his prophets in the Old Testament. He offers God his cooperation in keeping the mystery of the Incarnation secret; in his capacity as representative of the Eternal Father, he constantly recalls to our minds, in his ministry toward the Holy Child, the awareness of His divinity. By the tasks that he fulfills, he prevents us from forgetting that Jesus is true God and Son of the true God. So even while teaching us the sweetest familiarity toward Jesus, he also teaches us the most profound respect. On the one hand, he encourages us to draw near and to come and kiss the feet of Jesus; on the other, he bids us fall to our knees and worship the Newborn Eternal One (Father Faber).

The Miraculous Spring of Mount Bessillon

On June 7, 1660, while Louis XIV, King of France, was at the Spanish frontier to meet the infanta Marie-Thérèse, the new Queen of France, a shepherd—one Gaspard Ricard d'Estienne—in the middle of a scorching day, took refuge with his animals in the shade of the trees of Mount Bessillon in the heart of the department of the Var, in the commune of Cotignac.[1] He was suffering from thirst, as he had long since drained his flask. Suddenly, a man of imposing stature appeared before him and, pointing to a rock, said to him: "I am Joseph. Lift this rock and you shall drink." Gaspard estimated from its appearance the weight of the enormous rock, and replied simply: "I won't be able to; it's far too heavy." But the mysterious visitor repeated his order. Then the shepherd approached and, to his great astonishment, overturned the rock at his first try. Another surprise: clear water began to gush out from the spot. Gaspard threw himself upon the water as it flowed and drank eagerly. When he raised himself up to express both his astonishment and his gratitude, the man had vanished.

The shepherd ran to give the news to the village, where naturally nobody was willing to believe him. But in the end, some of the people decided to follow him to the place where everybody knew there would be no spring. On their arrival they shouted with joy, for the water was flowing in plenty, and had already been doing so for three hours. Everyone observed that the rock which Gaspard had shifted so easily by himself only moved with the combined efforts of eight men. Then it was that Gaspard became aware of the power given him from Heaven, and cried: "It was St. Joseph who was there; it is certainly he who

1. Cf. Mgr Barthe, Bishop of Fréjus, in *Église de Fréjus-Toulon*, 1971, no. 3.

gave me the power to do it." All followed his example, threw themselves on their knees, and gave thanks to St. Joseph. Afterwards the cures obtained by applying this miraculous water drew crowds to Mount Bessillon. The devotion to St. Joseph, hitherto non-existent in that region, took on an extraordinary expansion, and very quickly spread beyond Provence.

With the gifts that the pilgrims placed near the spring or sent to the inhabitants of Cotignac, the elders of the village decided, with the approval of the Bishop of Fréjus, to build over the spring a chapel in honor of St. Joseph.

Little time elapsed before these facts become known as far away as Paris, where the name of Cotignac has remained significant since the time of Louis XIII's vow. Then took place the pious deed of Louis XIV on behalf of St. Joseph. Probably struck by the mysterious coincidence between his entering France from Spain with her whom he was to marry two days later, and the apparition of St. Joseph at Cotignac, the king, who already owed his very existence to Our Lady of Graces[2], could only agree to the joint entreaty of his mother and his wife, and decree that henceforward the feast of St. Joseph should be observed as a public holiday

2. At the request of the Most Blessed Virgin, a shrine was in fact built in 1519 on another hill, not far from Cotignac, under the title of Our Lady of Graces. The favors granted there by the Mother of God quickly drew crowds, all the more since Pope Leo X granted indulgences to the pilgrims by bull, thus recognizing the reality of the apparitions.

throughout the kingdom. Then, on March 19, 1661, the king consecrated France to St. Joseph, as his father had consecrated it to Mary twenty-three years earlier.[3]

Countless are all the graces gained through the intercession of St. Joseph, especially in favor of married couples who, wishing to see their home gladdened by the presence of a child, address themselves to him with confidence and ask him to grant them the grace of fertility.

✠

St. Joseph

[F. W. Faber (1814-63)]

Hail, holy Joseph, hail!
Husband of Mary, hail!
Chaste as the lily flower
In Eden's peaceful vale.

Hail, holy Joseph, hail!
Father of Christ esteemed,
Father be thou to those
Thy foster-Son redeemed.

---

3. At the time of the French Revolution, the shrine of Our Lady of Graces was plundered and demolished. It was rebuilt in 1810, and today is served by a community of the Brothers of Saint John. The chapel of St. Joseph which had ceased to be maintained, has since 1978 been restored by a community of Benedictine nuns who use it as their convent chapel.

Hail, holy Joseph, hail!
Prince of the house of God,
May His blest graces be
By thy pure hands bestowed.

Hail, holy Joseph, hail!
Comrade of angels, hail:
Cheer thou the hearts that faint,
And guide the steps that fail.

Hail, holy Joseph, hail!
God's choice wert thou alone;
To thee the Word made flesh
Was subject as a Son.

Mother of Jesus, bless,
And bless, ye saints on high,
All meek and simple souls
That to St. Joseph cry. Amen.

In honor of St. Joseph

Be true to meditation of the mysteries of the faith by daily recitation of the Holy Rosary.

NINTH DAY

A Holy Marriage

What were the thoughts of Mary and Joseph on being united under the eyes of God? Ah! They were surely turned toward the Christ who was to come, toward the promised Messiah. The expectation of the Messiah was in the heart of every good Israelite. The Patriarchs, on entering into marriage, had in view primarily the propagation of the race from which the Messiah was to come.

But Mary had promised God to remain a virgin, and that promise was very dear to her. She agreed to marry Joseph, but she would remain a virgin. And behold, St. Joseph came into the presence of Mary. At once, enlightened by the Holy Spirit, by a sweet unction, his most pure soul understands that Mary must remain a virgin, that virginity is essential to her person, inseparable from her. Mary inspires only chaste thoughts. She can be loved only with a virginal love. From the first, Joseph is won to the zeal of holy virginity; and their marriage is made on the understanding that they will entrust one another with their virginity. The virginity of Mary will be the treasure of Joseph, as the virginity of Joseph will be the treasure of Mary. What Joseph loves most in Mary is that she is a virgin, so all his love for her consists in guarding very preciously her virginity.

O, who can tell the delights of such a union which is not of the earth? The two souls of Mary and Joseph meet and melt into one another in the ineffable light of a wholly divine fusion, breathing the spiritual perfumes of holy virginity.

Virginity is the law of this marriage; a marriage, however, is called to bear fruit. "That fruit," says St. Augustine, "God gives in the Person of His own Son taking flesh in the womb of Mary." In the hidden designs of God, the union of the two spouses prepared for the coming of the Messiah. Now, the Messiah becomes their Child. Yes, affirms the great Doctor, St. Augustine, Jesus can rightly be called the fruit of the virginal marriage of Mary and Joseph; He is given, not separately to Mary, but to her and to her spouse, to be theirs together.

St. Joseph was not informed immediately of the Incarnation of the Son of God in his chaste spouse, because she stands ahead of him in election and holiness. Furthermore, the perplexity of Joseph was to serve as witness to the virginal conception of the Saviour. Consider the words of the angel to St. Joseph. He does not give him rights over the Child, rights which he could not have; he simply informs him that Mary has conceived by the Holy Spirit, and that she remains his spouse in her Divine Maternity. The bond of marriage is not destroyed by the intervention of the Holy Spirit, who gives it its fruit; it is strengthened by the coming of the Divine Child.

Joseph was the Spouse of the Virgin Mary; now he is the Spouse of the Mother of God. He is invited to exercise the right of a father over the Child by giving Him His name, Jesus.

O Joseph, Spouse of the Mother of God! What dazzling greatness is concealed in that matchless title! And that greatness springs from the exquisite purity of your soul. You are the Spouse of the Virgin Mother of God, because you are a virgin yourself, a virgin in soul and body. Ah! Obtain for us something of that celestial purity which made you so great, yet which left you so humble (Dom Bernard Maréchaux).

Novena of Masses and a Baby Saved from Abortion

One day, a young woman, mother of three children, presented herself at the Convent of the Religious of St. Joseph at Bessillon, asking them to pray earnestly with her. In fact, she was expecting a fourth child and was herself affected by a serious illness. The doctors had given up hope and told her that the only way that she could pull through was to have an abortion, even adding that this was for her a duty as she already had three children to bring up. Faced with this advice which she could not follow, she went to find a priest, who said to her: "Go for nine days to Mass at St. Joseph's Convent at Bessillon."

She obeyed at once and, ill as she was, she managed to travel more than one hundred and fifty kilometers during nine consecutive days, to come and make her supplication to St. Joseph at the place of his apparition.

The child was born at full term, with no defects. In fact, he is a fine boy of eleven and a half years (1993), very intelligent and full of life. He has been followed by two little brothers. The three of them make a happy trio.

Despair Turned into Hope

On another occasion, the nuns of Mount Bessillon received a telephone call from someone who did not make himself known and left them this message: "I am on the verge of disaster—financial, moral and spiritual—and deeply depressed. Please pray to St. Joseph for me."

Three years later, the same man wrote to them to say: "I have emerged from my darkness; I have found a situation that I enjoy; my wife has come back to me and is expecting a third child; together, we are discovering how much the good God loves us, He who has come to look for us in our misery. Give thanks to St. Joseph with us."

✢

Prayer to St. Joseph, Guardian of the Holy Family

Blessed Joseph, husband of Mary, be with us this day.
Thou didst protect and cherish the Virgin;
loving the Child Jesus as thy Son,
thou didst rescue Him from the danger of death.
Defend the Church, the household of God,
purchased by the blood of Christ.
Guardian of the Holy Family,
be with us in our trials.
May thy prayers obtain for us
the strength to flee from error
and wrestle with the powers of corruption,
so that in life we may grow in holiness
and in death rejoice in the crown of victory. Amen.

In honor of St. Joseph

Have a deep love for the holy virtue of purity and avoid dangerous occasions, especially indecent shows. Keep control of the eyes. "There will be fashions which will greatly offend Our Lord" (Our Lady of Fatima).

TENTH DAY

The Earthly Trinity

It is not in the power of mortal tongue to express the immense honor to which our saint was elevated when She who appeared in the world like dawn breaking was given to him as spouse, She whose ever-increasing virtues grew into a rich dowry which She brought to Joseph, her husband. The august Virgin wanted no other provision in the marriage agreement except that her spouse be altogether like her, both in chastity and in purity of soul; and if the agreement was in a sense the work of the Holy Spirit Himself, who can doubt that the Blessed Virgin's wish was granted and that Joseph was enriched with gifts, qualities and virtues similar to those of Mary? "God," says St. Bernardine of Siena, "could only unite to the soul of so great a Virgin one whose virtue and activity were so like hers."

The most beautiful prerogative of St. Joseph, as Spouse of Mary, is that he is considered and honored as the Head of the Holy Family, which one author did not hesitate to call the Earthly Trinity. Like the pious Gerson, "I would like to be eloquent enough to describe for you this wonderful trinity of Jesus, Mary and Joseph."

Jesus, Mary and Joseph were three. Nevertheless, they seem to be only one—one in a unity so marvelous, a unity which of three made only one, and nevertheless left them three. Pay, therefore, frequent honor to that trinity, that was visible for us on earth: Jesus, Mary and Joseph. Engrave in your heart in letters of gold those three heavenly names, utter them often, write them everywhere: *Jesus, Mary, Joseph*. Repeat them several times a day, those sacred names, and may they still be on your lips when you draw your last breath (St. Leonard of Port-Maurice).

★

★ ★

Who can doubt that it is our duty to honor St. Joseph, when the Son of God Himself honored him with the name of father?

And indeed the Evangelists do not hesitate to give him that name. *His father and mother were wondering*, says St. Luke, *at those things which were spoken concerning him.*[1] It is also the name the Divine Mother gave him: *Thy father and I have sought thee sorrowing.*[2]

---

1. *Lk* 2:33.
2. *Ibid.* 2:48.

If then the King of Kings wished to elevate Joseph to so high an honor, it is right and just that we try to honor him as much as we can.

"Which angel or saint," says St. Basil, "has ever deserved to be called father of the Son of God?" Joseph was more honored by God than all the Patriarchs, Prophets, Apostles and Pontiffs. They have the name of servants; Joseph has the name of father.

So St. Joseph as father is placed at the head of this little family, small in number, but great by the two great personages it contains: the Mother of God and the only Son of God made man. In this household, Joseph commands, and the Son of God obeys. "This subjection of the Son of God," says Gerson, "while proving to us the humility of the Saviour, shows us the high dignity of Joseph. And what greater dignity, what higher elevation could there be than to command the One who commands all the Kings?" (St. Alphonsus de Liguori)

"See You Soon, Philomena!"

Philomena, a girl of nineteen, had been confined to bed since September 5th with a nervous disorder. Pain and distress had sapped her strength to the point where any kind of movement had become unbearable and her stomach could not tolerate so much as a teaspoonful of broth. She had no alternative but to turn to God. All those who visited the sick girl prayed that the Lord would take pity on one who suffered so much and reward her resignation by putting an end to her martyrdom, summoning her young soul to the unending joys of Heaven.

Such was her sorry state when, on February 28th, Philomena received a letter from a nun, her former superior, exhorting her not to lose courage and to begin a novena to St. Joseph on the tenth day of the following month, so as to finish it on the feast day of the great patriarch. The confidence of the superior was so strong that the letter ended with these words: "My hope is so great that I dare say: Regards, see you on the 19th; I hope that, after God, you will visit me: St. Joseph is the patron of our house." Her confidence was shared by the sick girl who declared with conviction that she would be cured on the 19th.

During the course of the novena, her illness grew worse. On the 17th, she suffered terrible pains. On the 18th, she felt some relief. Then on the 19th she had the joy of receiving Holy Communion. A few minutes afterwards, she got up all of a sudden and knelt in front of an image of St. Joseph which was on a table a few steps away.

Her cure was as complete as it was instantaneous. All the symptoms disappeared, all without exception, and her weakened stomach could retain and digest the food that they gave her. All thanks to St. Joseph!

This One Is Signed

A community of nuns in the United States tells this story.

"Early in February, we placed a photograph of a small car, with a note saying why we needed it, by the statue of St. Joseph in our entrance. The month of March came without any answer, when, in the last week, on Wednesday, a gentleman phoned saying that he wanted to give us a car. He asked if a Sister could go with him to the dealer in order to bring the car home. When the dealer brought out the car, it was exactly the same model as the one in the photograph: a small, dark blue Ford.

"The car was blessed a few days later, and we had a Mass said in thanksgiving to St. Joseph. Did he not, in a way, sign his answer?"

✠

Cælitum, Joseph,
Hymn for Matins on the Feast of St. Joseph
(Monastic Breviary)

Friend of the angels in Paradise still,
Helpless humanity's refuge from ill,
Joseph, the worship and strength of our days,
Graciously hear us who sing to thy praise.

Chosen thou wert by thy Maker's decree
Spotless virginity's bridegroom to be;
Thee the Eternal His father would call,
Steward on earth of His bounty[3] to all.

Housed with the oxen He lay in the cold—
Kings had but dreamed of it, prophets foretold,
Thou thy Redeemer rejoicing didst see,
Father and worshipper, bending the knee.

Monarch of monarchs, whom worlds must obey—
Hell doth acknowledge him, bowed to His sway;
Heaven in its courses His word doth fulfil—
He became subject on earth to thy will.

Glory to God, Three in One, let us own,
Who 'mid the angels thy merits doth crown;
Would but He grant, through those merits, that we
Live everlastingly, Joseph, with thee. Amen.

In honor of St. Joseph

In union with St. Joseph, perform our duties in life with a greater spirit of faith and consecrate them to God by means of short and fervent prayers.

3. In Latin: "ministrum salutis"—minister or dispenser of salvation, that salvation which is the perfect expression of the Divine Bounty towards us.

ELEVENTH DAY

Temptation of St. Joseph

Joseph her husband, being a just man and not willing publicly to expose her, was minded to put her away privately.[1] It was right of Joseph not to accuse Mary since he was just. He would not have been just if he had concealed adultery, nor could he be just if he condemned one whom he knew to be innocent. Being just and unwilling to expose Mary publicly, he preferred to send her away privately.

Why did he want to send her away? Listen to this which is not my opinion, but that of the Fathers. The reason Joseph wanted to separate from Mary is the one invoked by St. Peter himself to avoid the Lord: *Depart from me, for I am a sinful man, O Lord*;[2] and by the centurion to keep Him from his house: *Lord, I am not worthy that thou shouldst enter under my roof.*[3] So it was with St. Joseph, too. Feeling himself to be unworthy and sinful, he thought: "She is so perfect and so great that I do

1. *Mt* 1:19.   2. *Lk* 5:8.   3. *Mt* 8:8.

not deserve that she should share her intimacy with me any longer; her astonishing dignity surpasses me and frightens me." He saw with sacred fear that she carried the clear marks of a divine presence. As he could not fathom the mystery, he preferred to leave her. Fear struck Peter at the greatness of the Lord's power; fear seized the Centurion at the majesty of His presence; fear seized St. Joseph quite naturally as it would any man at the uncanniness of the extraordinary miracle, at the depth of the mystery, and that is why he wanted to separate from her privately.

Can we be surprised that St. Joseph thought himself unworthy to live with the Blessed Virgin when we are told that even St. Elizabeth trembled with awe in her presence. Here are her words: *Whence is this to me, that the mother of my Lord should come to me?*[4]

That is why St. Joseph wanted to put her away; but why privately and not publicly? To avoid all inquiry into the motives for the separation and to escape the obligation of accounting for it. If he had given his opinion and the proof he had of the purity of Mary, the Jews would have derided him and stoned Mary. How would those Jews believe in the Truth still silent in His Mother's womb, when, later, they scorned His outcry in the temple? What would they have done to Christ, as yet invisible, when, later, they laid sacrilegious hands upon Him although He shone with the splendor of His

4. *Lk* 1:43.

miracles? In order not to be reduced to telling lies or to laying an innocent open to blame, it was quite right of St. Joseph, the just man, to separate from Our Lady in secret (St. Bernard).

When It's Worth Feeling Bad

A man of forty-seven years, consumed by greed, became ill with measles. He sought a place among the poor of a hospital. The religious Sister in charge of his room, approached him soon and asked whether he was a good Christian.

"Little does it matter," he responded rather rudely, "provided that I am an honest man."

"But being honest is not enough for getting into Heaven."

"I attend Mass on Sundays."

"There is still more needed. A good Christian has other duties."

The sick man, annoyed by this conversation, turned toward the wall and remained silent. The Sister withdrew, and since nothing indicated a serious condition, she made up her mind to await a better opportunity. She even postponed giving him a medal of St. Joseph, although the thought occurred to her several times.

Eventually, the condition of the man worsened as the fever increased and the illness spread to his chest. The chaplain arrived and tried to bring this poor man to Christian repentance. The unfortunate responded to his charitable attempts only with vulgarities and spat out all sorts of abuses against priests. The Sister in charge of the men's section entrusted this sinner to St. Joseph, and succeeded, although with difficulty, in placing the saint's medal around his neck. Soon the dying man, glad to have this pious object, asked to keep it for good, and even to carry it away if he should one day leave the hospital. From this time on a transformation took place within him. Respectful manners replaced the boorishness which had made him inaccessible, and when once more spoken to about confession, he did not resist but confessed most sincerely.

"O my good Sister," he said to the nun caring for him after his talk with the chaplain, "how happy I am! This time I confessed all my sins and I really felt very bad, it's true, but I feel such joy that it was worth it. How I regret having done my duty so badly in the past. If I recuperate with St. Joseph's protection, I shall live very differently."

The illness progressed rapidly. It was deemed essential to give him Extreme Unction, which he received in the most consoling dispositions. From then until the end of his life he edified those around him with his truly Christian attitude. "To die having done so much ill and so little good, how terrible it is," he remarked.

Half an hour before giving up his soul to God he was still totally conscious, and he repeated ever so touchingly: "My God, be merciful to me. . . . Holy

Mary, pray for me, a poor sinner. . . . St. Joseph, help me to die well." He expired without agony. We firmly hope that Heaven has taken his contrition into account.

More Than One Surprise

The customary September collection had to be omitted that year in Kerala—report the Little Sisters of the Poor from a house in Southern India. They had recourse to St. Joseph with great fervor and, with the immense confidence which all the Sisters of the Congregation share, asked him to settle matters, because the people of that state appreciate the good done for elderly people and are very generous.

Scarcely had the decision been made when our good St. Joseph began to send them surprises. One of the most unexpected was a gift of Rs. 20,000 ($1,400) from a person unknown to the Sisters.

Some time later, a person who had never heard of their house succeeded in selling his land for a good price. While speaking to an official in Kotagir, a town distant from the Sisters, he expressed his desire to do something for the poor. The official, who previously had worked in the Sisters' town, told him that he knew of an institution where his contribution would be put to good use. The benefactor visited them without telling the reason for his coming. Much impressed by the residents and by all he saw, he handed to the

Mother Superior, before leaving, a cheque for Rs. 10,000 ($700). When the Mother asked him what name she should write on the receipt, he answered: "Someone who wishes you well."

✠

Te, Joseph, Celebrent Agmina Cælitum,
Hymn for Vespers on the Feast of St. Joseph
(Monastic Breviary)

O Joseph, heavenly hosts thy worthiness proclaim,
And Christendom conspires to celebrate thy fame,
Thou who in purest bonds wert to the Virgin bound,
How glorious is thy name renowned.

Thou, when thou didst behold thy spouse, about to bear,
Wast sore oppressed with doubt, wert filled with wondering care.
At length the angel's word thy anxious heart relieved:
She by the Spirit hath conceived.

Thou with thy newborn Lord didst seek far Egypt's land,
As wandering pilgrims ye fled o'er the desert sand;
That Lord when lost, by thee is in the Temple found,
While tears are shed and joys abound.

Not till death's hour is passed do other men obtain
The meed of holiness and glorious rest attain;
Thou like to angels made, in life completely blest,
Didst clasp thy God unto thy breast.

O Holy Trinity, thy suppliant servants spare,
Grant us to rise to Heaven for Joseph's sake and prayer,
And so our grateful hearts to Thee shall ever raise
Exulting canticles of praise. Amen.

In honor of St. Joseph

Refrain from rash judgments which too easily lead us to looking down on others. It is better to entrust those persons to St. Joseph and to pray for them.

TWELFTH DAY

Trial and Temptation

Joseph arose at once and, following the command he had received, took the Child and His Mother and fled into Egypt. Let us consider the obedience of that just man and try to imitate it, for it includes the four degrees which constitute the perfection of that virtue.

– St. Joseph obeyed with total submission of judgment. At the first word of the angel, without replying, he accepted the divine command. He could have suggested to the Lord that there were easier ways to protect His Son. If the flight was necessary, why not go to Arabia or Samaria, instead of Egypt? But far from that upright heart was the least objection. Respectfully, St. Joseph submitted and was silent. The mission of the celestial ambassador toward him having been fulfilled, St. Joseph was not curious to know more. He asked no questions and followed, to the letter, the advice that the Holy Spirit gives in the *Book of Ecclesiasticus*: *Seek not the things that are too high for thee, and search not into things above thy ability; but the things that God hath commanded thee, think on them always, and in many of His works be not curious.*[1]

– St. Joseph obeyed with courage and magnanimity. It was very difficult to carry out the command. It meant leaving his home and country, giving up all contact with his relatives, going into exile in a foreign, faraway land, where he would be deprived of human assistance. His desire to carry out God's will made him generously sacrifice his own. Dare I say that his obedience surpassed that of Abraham? Although that holy patriarch went forth from his country and forgot his father's house to go where God called him, yet he brought with him great wealth, and many servants followed in his train.

– St. Joseph obeyed promptly and without delay. He did not go on sleeping until morning. He did not stay in bed the rest of the night. He got up at once, made known to his holy Spouse the revelation he had received from the angel and, without delay, taking nothing with them, they departed. Thus they were on their way before dawn, perfectly carrying out the command they were given to flee in secret, as the shades of night permitted them to do.

– Mary and Joseph obeyed with great joy. The days were long and tiring; they were deprived of

1. *Eccli* 3:22.

ordinary means which might alleviate the hardships of the journey. They hardly gave a thought to their wants. They felt an inner joy that made them insensible to care, absorbed as they were in these two thoughts: it is God's will that they suffer, and for them God's will is the surest consolation; and above all, they have with them the Divine Child. His sweet company did more than charm their loneliness and, in their abandonment, replaced all things they might have lacked. Hence they did not seek elsewhere the comforts and refreshment most travelers are so eager to obtain.

O Almighty God, who gave to Mary and Joseph a spirit of such perfect obedience, I beg You through their merits to grant me the same spirit, so that I may obey You like them with complete submission of judgment, with courage, promptness and joy, desiring only to do Your will and fully confident that Your Divine Providence will never forsake me as long as I shall persevere in uniting my will to Yours (Venerable Louis de Ponte).

Back Home Safe and Sound

During the Franco-Prussian war (1870), after the bloody battle of Patay, an unhappy mother, whose son was a soldier in the French army, went into a church. Her husband had just told her the bad news: the Prussian Army had refused a pass to a lady they knew who wanted to visit the battlefield in order to collect her husband's remains. "Alas," said the poor mother, "if our child should die, we won't even have the consolation of giving him a decent burial." The anguished mother came in tears to kneel before Immaculate Mary; after a few moments of prayer, she got up and went to the altar of St. Joseph, where she knelt and again shed many tears. All of a sudden, with the bravery and hope that a mother's love inspires, she took her son's picture from her pocket and slid it behind the statue of the holy patriarch. "Bring him back to me, St. Joseph," she cried.

St. Joseph heard the cry of the devoted mother. On March 19, 1871, the young man, safe and sound, came home to his family. In fulfillment of a sacred vow, the mother of this young man protected by St. Joseph had a white, marble ex-voto placed in the chapel where she had wept and prayed, with these words on it: "Glory to good St. Joseph, who preserved a beloved son for his family during the war of 1870 and brought him back safe and sound on March 19, 1871." That is how St. Joseph, having experienced sorrow in his life on earth, knows how to console the grieving hearts who implore his protection.

A Mother's Heroic Sacrifice

During the same war, a young man belonging to a devout family in Northern France was enlisted in the militia of his department. His mother, distressed by his departure, commended him with tears to the patron saint of families and even offered God the sacrifice of her own life if it would safeguard her son's. St. Joseph watched over the young man and, after many dangers and hardships, on March 18th, the eve of his feast day, brought him back to his good and loving mother whose heart overflowed with joy and gratitude. Alas! Her happiness was short-lived. The young man came home sick and suffering and, eight days after his arrival, developed small-pox so severe that the doctors had little hope of saving him. His mother took care of him and, to secure his cure through St. Joseph's intercession, she renewed the offering she had made. "Dear Lord," she said, "accept my own life and save my son's." She was heard. The young man recovered, but the poor mother caught the small-pox and, within a few days, was at death's door. She died on April 24, a victim of her love and devotion.

✝

Hymn to the Guardian of Mary

Dear Guardian of Mary, fond guide of her Child!
Life's ways are full weary, the desert is wild,
Bleak sands are all 'round us, no home can we see;
Sweet Spouse of our Lady! we lean upon thee.

For thou to the pilgrim art father and guide,
And Jesus and Mary felt safe at thy side;
Ah! blessed St. Joseph, how safe should I be,
Sweet Spouse of our Lady! if thou wert with me.

O blessed St. Joseph! how great was thy worth;
The one chosen shadow of God upon earth;
The Father of Jesus—ah, then wilt thou be,
Sweet Spouse of our Lady! a father to me?

When the treasures of God were unsheltered on earth,
Safe keeping was found for them both in thy worth;
O Father of Jesus! be father to me,
Sweet Spouse of our Lady! and I will love thee. Amen.

In honor of St. Joseph

Gladly accept the trials God sends us and bear them cheerfully without complaining.

THIRTEENTH DAY

The Flight into Egypt

The Holy Magi having notified Herod of the birth of the King of the Jews, that barbarous prince gave orders to kill all male children up to two years old in the vicinity of Bethlehem. As God wished for the time being to preserve His Son from death, He sent an Angel to warn St. Joseph to take the Child and His Mother and flee into Egypt.

Consider here the prompt obedience of St. Joseph who, even though the angel had not set a time for his departure, made no difficulties either about the time or about the manner of such a trip or where he would stay in Egypt, but made ready to depart. He immediately told Mary.

What must have been the grief of Joseph on this journey when he saw his beloved spouse, not used to so much walking, suffer so, carrying in her arms that dear Child whom they held in turn as they fled, in constant apprehension of meeting Herod's soldiers at every turn of the road; and all of this in the hardest part of winter with the discomfort of wind and snow! What had they to eat during the trip? A piece of bread they had brought with them or whatever they might receive as alms. At night they had no place to rest except some wretched hut or an open field under the stars, with, at best, a tree for shelter. St. Joseph was indeed resigned to the will of the Eternal Father, which was that His only Son should suffer even from infancy to expiate the sins of the human race; but it broke Joseph's heart to hear Jesus cry because of the cold and the damp.

Finally, consider how much St. Joseph had to suffer during those seven years he spent in Egypt, in the midst of an idolatrous, barbarian and unknown nation, having no friends or relatives to help him. St. Bernard said that St. Joseph had to work day and night to provide food for his wife and for the Child who Himself provides food for all men and for all animals on earth (St. Alphonsus de Liguori).

⋆
⋆ ⋆

The angel ordered him to set out immediately and to take Our Lady and her beloved Son into Egypt. He set off at once without saying a word. He did not ask: "Where shall I go? What road shall I take? What will we eat? Who will shelter us?" He set out bravely, carrying his tools on his back, with the hope of earning the living of the whole family by the sweat of his brow. O! How much that tedium, that inner weariness of which we spoke, must have weighed upon him! The Angel had not even told him how long he was to stay there; he could not establish a residence, not knowing when he might be ordered to return. How long would he stay in Egypt? The angel did not tell him, nor did he ask. Actually he stayed there a long time, never enquiring about his return, assured as he was that the one who gave him notice of his departure would do the same for his coming back, and he was ready to obey him once more. He was not only in a foreign country, but in one unfriendly to the Israelites; for the Egyptians had not forgotten how their departure had been the cause for which, having gone in their pursuit, a large part of the Egyptians were drowned in the Red Sea.

You can imagine how eager St. Joseph was to come back, on account of the constant anxiety he felt among the Egyptians. The worry of not knowing when he might leave must have tormented his poor heart; he remained, nonetheless, always the same: meek, calm and perseverant in his submission to the will of the God who led him. For as he is truly called just, so his will was ever adjusted to the will of God, in union and conformity with it.

To be just is simply to be in perfect union with the will of God and to conform to it in all events, in prosperity or adversity. No one can doubt that St. Joseph was perfectly obedient to God at all times and occasions. Do you not see it? See how the Angel orders him around. He tells him to go to Egypt, and he goes. He tells him to come back, and he comes back (St. Francis de Sales).

Patron of the Unborn

Here is a mother's testimony to the faithfulness of St. Joseph toward those who call on him for all their needs.

"March 19, 19...

"Dear Brothers,

"Today, March 19, Feast of St. Joseph, I am happy to tell you that this great saint has answered my prayers once again.[1] I have been praying since the first of this month and, every day, he gave me help and courage to accept the painful situation in which I was living.

"Then yesterday, while I was praying to St. Joseph with complete trust, my parents came to visit me. They had not spoken to me for weeks, not since the day I told them I was pregnant. The little child I have been carrying for the last three months was for them an inconvenience, as also for my husband and the rest of my family. The child was not welcome.

"Silently, I asked St. Joseph to help me bear this suffering, this hostility, and begged that he would soften the hearts of those near and dear to me.

"Last night, on the eve of St. Joseph's feast, my parents appeared at my house and asked if they

1. This mother had previously prayed a novena to St. Joseph to obtain a great grace, and the saint had shown his generosity by granting her more than she had asked for.

could stay for dinner. I was happy to greet them and made them fully welcome. At the end of the meal, as they were leaving, they invited me and my husband to spend Sunday with them so that we could visit with all the family, and added how much they would be pleased to have us. I could read in their eyes their regret and shame at having wished the death of my child, threatened by so many close relatives who wanted it to be aborted.

"I believed then that St. Joseph had touched their hearts, and I was deeply moved. So many times Jesus' foster-father, who is ours too, had been lavish with his graces. He always sustained me in my most difficult times, in my daily work as well as in my private life.

"Knowing how much you love and honor St. Joseph as your patron, I wanted you to know about this special grace given to me.

"I had confided to you my family problems and my difficult situation. I owe to you, to all of you, this grace; and now I am waiting for the greatest of saints after Mary to bring back to God all those sinners who despair because they have no faith.

"That is the grace that I wish for my dear ones, so that their souls and hearts may be in peace and harmony with God the Father Almighty in union with the Holy Spirit for all eternity."

✠

Prayer to St. Joseph for Unborn Children

Good St. Joseph, Spouse of the Blessed Virgin Mary and Protector of Our Lord Jesus Christ, we beseech thee to protect the lives of all unborn children who are in danger of abortion.

Through thy care and guidance, instill in the hearts and minds of mothers and fathers that the innocent unborn are human beings who are worthy of life and the benefits of parental love.

Great St. Joseph, let thy strong arms surround these children, shield them from harm and grant them the joy of life. Grant them above all the support needed for the reception of the Sacrament of Baptism by which they may become children of God and heirs to eternal life. Amen.

In honor of St. Joseph

Have great confidence in the paternal goodness of St. Joseph and really entrust all our cares to him.

FOURTEENTH DAY

A Sublime Favor

Let us not think that the title of "Father" given to St. Joseph is one devoid of an underlying reality. Joseph gives an order and it is obeyed by Him who made daybreak and the sun and whom the morning stars adore. He speaks and before him bows that Divine Child at whose name every knee should bow in Heaven, on earth and under the earth[1] : that God whose omnipotent voice shatters the cedar trees[2] and creates anew or dismays all nature at His will. Attentive to the needs of this earthly father, He anticipates his wishes, helps him in his work, comforts him in his sorrows.

Such was, however, and such, I dare say, had to be the conduct of Jesus Christ Our Lord towards St. Joseph. He who had come to fulfill the law strictly, He who even in pagan princes and governors respected the power that had been given to them from above, was far from failing in obligations drawn from nature and from which even God will not

1. Cf. *Phil* 2:10

2. Cf. *Ps* 28:5.

dispense. Well may St. John the Evangelist make known to all mankind that he had the happiness of leaning once on Jesus' bosom; for him that was a favor, but it was a right for Joseph. Moreover, what happened only once to the beloved disciple, happened a thousand times either when Joseph in his old age tasted sweet refreshment in the protection of the Divine Saviour, or when Jesus in His childhood lovingly rested on Joseph.

Now Joseph had a far greater favor. He had the first and the best share in the chalice of his Son and in the afflictions which exalted Him. That seems surprising at first, for it means that God's love can be measured by the greatness of the sufferings He gives to His elect. It is only natural, however, considering that crosses are the portion of the saints, that the road to Heaven is paved with tears and tribulations and that those who are most loved are also most sorely tried. Joseph is one of those just men who walked the highway of piety and religion without gathering flowers except in the midst of thorns, and whose virtue Our Lord was pleased to test by the most vexing and unsettling trials.

Ite ad Joseph, et quidquid dixerit vobis facite—Go to Joseph, and do all that he shall say to you,[3] said Pharaoh to those of his subjects who were beginning to feel the effects of famine and poverty.

Ite ad Joseph. Go to Joseph, you whom the want of spiritual goods has reduced to the most wretched poverty; before long you will meet with abundance.

3. *Gen* 41:55.

Ite ad Joseph, et quidquid dixerit vobis facite. Go to Joseph, you who in prayer feel only dryness and distaste. Let anyone who does not know how to pray go to that great master and he will be well taught.

Ite ad Joseph. Go to Joseph, you who intending to follow in the footsteps of the God of virgins, feel in this body of death the rebellion of the flesh and the shameful outbursts of concupiscence.

Ite ad Joseph. Go to Joseph, you who are still unsure that you belong to God, you who because of some slight trouble are ready to leave His service and return to the world, and you will learn from his steadfastness how to stand firm amid the storms that would drive you from the path of virtue.

Ite. Go to him, you who are his Son's ministers. You owe him part of the substance of Christ Himself Who nourishes you with His Body; and His adorable Blood was formed with St. Joseph's toil and sweat.

Go to him, finally, all of you who want to be Christians not in name only but in deed. Not only will you find in him a powerful protector, but you will discover, too, a model of that strong, tender and grateful love which is the whole of the law and the essence of Christianity (Father Collet, Priest of the Mission).

A Guide amidst the Waves

Two Franciscan Fathers were sailing off the coast of Flanders when a violent storm sprang up sinking their ship with its three hundred passengers. The two friars clung to a piece of wood from the ship and thus kept afloat on the waves. In that terrible situation they entrusted themselves to St. Joseph and remained for three days between life and death. At last, on the third day, the saint came to their assistance. He appeared to them in the form of a young man full of grace and majesty, standing on the plank they clung to. He greeted them in a manner so friendly that it filled their hearts with unutterable consolation and imparted miraculous strength to their limbs, after which, acting as pilot, he guided them through the waters and brought them ashore.

"I am Joseph," he said. "If you wish to please me, recite the *Our Father* and the *Hail Mary* seven times, in memory of the seven sorrows and seven joys which I experienced when living on earth in the company of Jesus and Mary."[4] Having said this, he disappeared, leaving the two friars full of joy and gratitude.

A Blue-tiled Bathroom

Nothing is impossible for St. Joseph. However, he enjoys trying his faithful to see how far their courage and perseverance in praying to him will go.

Here is an example:

"June 1992: 'Go to Joseph.'

"Thank you, O good St. Joseph! I had for a long time been looking for a more convenient house. . . .

4. Cf. a formula of this prayer pp. 244-247.

On the first of April, I had to leave the one in which I was living. On March 30th, we were still in our house with nothing new in sight. I was afraid of being thrown out into the street with my child. In my request to St. Joseph, I had asked for another residence with two bedrooms, a living room, kitchen, garden and if possible, a blue-tiled bathroom.

"On that evening, news came of someone moving from a house located in the heart of the town. Without too much hope, I hastened to the place.

"To my surprise, however, I was the first applicant to arrive. Accompanied by the owner, I inspected the house. Everything was to my taste: a spacious dining room, a kitchen, three bedrooms and a garden. I had yet to see the bathroom. There the greatest surprise was awaiting me—it was blue-tiled, exactly as I wanted!

"Thank you, O St. Joseph! This is a most marvelous grace obtained through your intercession. A statue of St. Joseph will be placed in our new dwelling. I shall ever persevere in prayer and never will I forget this particular favor!"

+

Prayer of St. Alphonsus to St. Joseph

O Holy Patriarch, I rejoice with thee at the exalted dignity by which thou wert deemed worthy to act as father to Jesus, to give Him orders and to be obeyed by Him Whom Heaven and earth obey. O great Saint, as thou wert served by a God, I too wish to be taken into thy service. I choose thee after Mary, to be my chief Advocate and Protector. I promise to honor thee every day by some special act of devotion and by placing myself under thy daily protection. By that sweet company which Jesus and Mary gave thee in thy lifetime, protect me all through life, so that I may never separate myself from my God by losing His grace. My dear St. Joseph, pray to Jesus for me. Certainly, He can never refuse thee anything, as He obeyed all thy orders while on earth. Tell Him to detach me from all creatures and from myself, to inflame me with His holy love, and then to do with me what He pleases. By that assistance which Jesus and Mary gave thee at death, I beg of thee to protect me in a special way at the hour of my death, so that dying assisted by thee, in the company of Jesus and Mary, I may go to thank thee in Paradise and, in thy company, to praise my God for all eternity. Amen.

Glory be, etc. three times.

In honor of St. Joseph

In imitation of St. Joseph, strive to grow in humility, meekly accepting humiliations, failure, ridicule and criticism, in order to be more like Jesus, meek and humble of heart.

FIFTEENTH DAY

The Love of St. Joseph for Jesus and Mary

Prior to his wedding, Joseph was already a saintly man, but once married to the Holy Virgin, he progressed much more in holiness. The way of life of his spouse was sufficient to sanctify him. As St. Bernardine of Siena says: If Mary is the sole channel of all graces granted to men, how much more must have her presence enriched her husband whom she loved so much, and who loved her so much in return.

Do we not have still greater reason to believe that the sanctity of Joseph increased because of his continuous dealings and intimacy with Jesus all the time they lived together?

If the two disciples on their way to Emmaus felt the glow of Divine Love in the short time they accompanied the Saviour and listened to Him, what lively flames of holy charity must have burned in the heart of Joseph for having conversed over thirty years with Our Lord Jesus, for having heard His words of life eternal, and having witnessed the marvelous examples of humility, patience and obedience which He gave by being very prompt to help him in all his works, and to serve him in everything needed within the house!

What fire of Divine Love must have been created by all of these marks of charity within the heart of Joseph, this heart which was detached from all earthly affections! It is true that he loved Mary very much, but his love for her in no way divided his heart. No, the heart of Joseph was not divided, because that love he had for his spouse filled his heart more and more with Divine Love. There is no doubt that simply living with Jesus of itself increased the merits and sanctity of St. Joseph to a point where we can say that he exceeded the merits of all the other saints.

Consider firstly the love of Joseph for his holy spouse. She was indeed the most beautiful lady of all creation; yet, she was the most humble, kind, pure, obedient and closest in love to God that ever existed among men and angels. Thus she deserved the entire love of Joseph who cherished virtue so much. In addition, Joseph saw how much he was loved by Mary who certainly loved him more than any other creature. He regarded her as the beloved of God, chosen to be the Mother of His only Son. Therefore, consider the affection held in the heart of the just and grateful Joseph for such a lovable wife.

Secondly, consider the love Joseph had for Jesus. When God chose this saint as the foster-father of

Jesus, He must have engraved in his heart the innate love of a father, the father of so lovable a Son, the father of an Infant God. Thus, the love of Joseph was not merely human, as is the love of other fathers, but surpassed the human level and led him to discern in the same Person, both a Son and a God. Joseph was well aware, through the divine revelation of the Angel, that this Child that he foresaw to be always with him, was indeed the Divine Word who, for the love of men, and in particular for himself, became incarnate. He knew that he had been chosen over all others to be the guardian of the Child's life, this Child who wanted to be called his Son. Well, then, consider what type of fire the Holy Love must have lit up in the heart of Joseph when he thought of all this, and when he saw his Divine Master serving him as an apprentice, sometimes opening or closing the shop, sometimes helping to cut wood or handle the plane and the axe, sometimes picking up or sweeping wood chips—in other words, obeying him submissively to the extent of doing nothing else unless authorized by His father.

The familiarity of those who love each other sometimes cools that love, because the more they get to know each other, the more they become aware of the other's deficiencies. This was not the case for St. Joseph. The more he conversed with Jesus, the more he became acquainted with His sanctity. Let us conclude from this point how much he loved Jesus! (St. Alphonsus de Liguori)

A New Home for the Elderly

Chile's 1985 earthquake destroyed the convent of the Little Sisters of the Poor, in Santiago, near Our Lady of Lourdes Basilica. Soon after, the Mother Superior General paid a visit to Chile.

The old persons evacuated from the ruined home were, for the most part, moved to another home in Santiago, while the remainder were housed in a number of other institutions. They prayed earnestly for the reconstruction of their home in Santiago. This situation soon became unbearable, and a large delegation came to petition the Mother Superior General for the rebuilding of their house. The Cardinal of Santiago strongly supported their request.

After praying and consulting the General Council, it was decided to go ahead with the plan of reconstruction, making an act of total confidence in St. Joseph, agent of Divine Providence. Two months later, in a manner completely unexpected, a donation of great importance was offered for this project. This unexpected sum allowed them to pay for the work, and on August 30, 1992, the house was inaugurated.

Saved from the Flood

"The heavy rains which had fallen since morning caused floods in the early afternoon in a southern quarter of a city in the United States. Rivers overflowed, sewers were blocked up, so much so that the water inundated the streets—transforming them into rivers—and invaded the cellars; families had to evacuate their homes. The electricity and telephone lines were cut until the next day; the airport had to be closed.

"In the street in front of our apartment the water reached 36 inches (90 cm) high. . . .

"In our apartment, the cellar was flooded and, for safety reasons, the elevators were put out of service. Once again, St. Joseph responded to our confidence: shortly after placing his statue outside and another on the windowsill with a small candle at his feet, the water level began to recede. . . . and finally the rains ceased."

Brief but touching, this letter demonstrates how much the Little Sisters of the Poor know how to be grateful towards their powerful protector, trying by this means to transmit their faith to the humble souls who confide in divine grace rather than in their own strength.

St. Joseph

(R. A. Knox)

Joseph, the scriptures love to trace
The glories of thy kingly line;
Yet no succession of thy race,
No long posterity was thine—
Of her the everlasting spouse
Who must a Virgin ever be,
The faithful ruler of His house
Who owns no fatherhood in thee.

There were no songs of old renown,
No crowds to greet you when you came,
Two wanderers, to your native town,
That lost inheritance to claim;
But hard the hearts, and cold the air,
And mean the lodging where you lay,
And long the exile you must bear
Till upstart Herod's dying day.

And though thy Son were God indeed,
Over that home no angels sang,
But still, through years of toil and need,
Hammer and mallet bravely rang;
And surely 'twas a gracious thing
When, standing at His father's knee,
The world's great Craftsman and its King
Not king but craftsman learned to be.

But, king or craftsman, die we must:
Who would not change his lot with thine,
In such sweet peace and holy trust
His earthly being to resign?
With Mary's comfort at thy side
Thy spirit, freed from mortal clay,
Out of God's presence satisfied
Into God's presence passed away.

Joseph, the Church of God protect;
Her priests with holy care endow;
Shield of the virgin-souls elect,
Hope of the fatherless, be thou:
And, when our parting spirits cling
To earthly joys that cannot bide,
Make Nazareth in our homes, and bring
Jesus and Mary to our side. Amen.

In honor of St. Joseph

Sanctify our love for those we cherish by loving them for the sake of Our Lord rather than for ourselves.

SIXTEENTH DAY

The Simplicity of St. Joseph

God ordered the just St. Joseph to receive the Blessed Virgin as his faithful wife, even though her condition seemingly accused her; to accept as his own Son a Child with whom he had nothing in common except the home they shared; to honor as his God the One to whom he was obliged to serve as protector and guardian. In these three circumstances, where such delicate sentiments do not come naturally, it is only an extreme simplicity that can render the heart obedient and accommodating. How did St. Joseph proceed? With regard to his holy Spouse, never were his suspicions more moderate nor doubt more respectful; nevertheless, he was so just that he could not have been made fully aware without Heaven becoming involved. Thus, an angel announced to him on behalf of God that she had conceived by the Holy Spirit. If his intentions had been less honorable, if he had belonged only partly to God, he would not have totally surrendered himself. In the deepest part of his soul there would have remained a hint of suspicion, and his affection for the Blessed Virgin would have forever been tinged with doubt and fear. But his heart, which sought God in total simplicity, knowing nothing else but complete unity with Him, had absolutely no difficulty in recognizing that the incorruptible virtue of his holy Spouse deserved the testimony of Heaven. His faith surpassed Abraham's, even though in the Scriptures the latter is depicted as the model of perfect faith and is praised in the Old Testament for having believed in the child-bearing of a sterile woman. Joseph believed that of a virgin, and he recognized in simplicity this great and impenetrable mystery of the virginal conception.

What is even more admirable, O St. Joseph, is that God desired you to receive as your own Son this Child of Mary's purity. You will not share with this Virgin the honor of being the natural parent, because her virginity would have been tainted; but you shall share the cares, vigilance and worries which were hers as she raised this precious Son. You will become the father of this holy Child, who has no father on earth, and even though you are not father by nature, you must become so through affection.

How then will such great works be accomplished? Where will he find this paternal heart if nature does not provide him with it? Can such inclinations be acquired by choice, and would we not worry in his place about false emotions and artificial affections? No, have no fear; the heart which seeks the Lord in simplicity is like clay which is soft and moldable and takes the form God wishes to mold it into; what God desires comes to it naturally. If therefore it is the desire of our Heavenly Father that St. Joseph replace Him in this world, and that he serve as father to His Son, then he will feel the natural inclinations, all the sweet emotions, all the tender affections of a paternal heart for this holy and Divine Child.

Indeed, during those three days when the Son of God slipped away to remain in the temple with the elders, Joseph was as affected as the Mother herself, and of this she was quite aware: *Pater tuus et ego dolentes quærebamus te*: *Thy father and I have sought Thee sorrowing.*[1] She associates him with her in the experience of sorrows. She has no apprehension here in calling him "Thy father," and does not pretend to contradict the holiness of His birth; it is because of his cares and worries that she says "Thy father," because he truly has paternal worries. See how this holy man takes upon himself the feelings God wants him to have with simplicity and good faith.

But, loving Jesus Christ as his Son, can he at the same time revere Him as his God? Without a doubt, but there would have been nothing more difficult had holy simplicity not made his spirit so docile as to surrender willingly to divine order (Bossuet).

1. *Lk* 2:48.

"I Knew How To Live; I'll Know How To Die"

In the midst of a plague that was devastating an entire country, and which was particularly affecting the poor, a charitable priest entered into a lowly and damp stable where a victim of the epidemic was suffering. What did he see? A dying old man, stretched out over disgusting rags. He was alone; a stack of hay served as his bed. Not a piece of furniture, not even a chair, for he had sold everything in the first days of his illness to buy some drops of soup. On bare, black walls hung a hatchet and two saws, which, along with his two arms—at least when he was able to move them—constituted his entire fortune. But now he had no energy to even lift them.

"Have courage, my friend," the confessor said to him. "It is a great grace which the Lord grants you today. You are about to depart from this world where you have known only sorrow."

"Sorrow!" the dying man exclaimed in a very faint voice. "You are wrong! I took St. Joseph as my patron saint and model and, like him, I have never complained of my lot. I knew neither hate nor envy; my sleep was peaceful. I worked hard by day, but I rested by night. The tools you see provided me with the bread I ate with delight. I was poor, it is true, but St. Joseph was just as poor; and I have kept fairly well up to now. If I recover, which I doubt, I shall return to my workplace and continue to bless the hand of God who, up to now, has taken care of me."

The priest, astounded, was not quite sure how to respond. However, he added:

"My friend, even if life has not been all that bad, you must nonetheless be resigned to leave it, because one must submit to the will of God."

"I knew how to live," replied the dying man, in a firm voice, "I'll know how to die. I bless the Lord for having given me life and for allowing me to pass through death in order to reach Him. I feel the time is at hand; here it is, so good-bye, Father!"

In this manner lived and died, full of peace, this devout worker, this just man, who had taken St. Joseph for his patron saint and model. Let us also during this month and always, be imitators of this great saint.

+

Liturgical Prayer

(Secret from the Votive Mass in Honor of St. Joseph)

Supported by the patronage of the Spouse of Thy most holy Mother, we beseech Thy clemency, O Lord, that Thou wouldst make our hearts despise all earthly things, and love Thee, the true God, with perfect charity. Thou who art God, living and reigning with God the Father in the unity of the Holy Spirit, world without end. Amen.

In honor of St. Joseph

Refrain from judging one's superiors, and recommend them to the Lord.

SEVENTEENTH DAY

The Chastity of St. Joseph

The spirit in St. Joseph was submitted to God in perfect justice, which, actually identified with charity and adorned with the gift of wisdom, made him feel and follow the will of God in all things and made him admirably docile to the guidance of the Holy Spirit. Subsequently, the flesh, in this chosen one of God, was particularly submissive to the spirit: Joseph the just was the most chaste among men.

There is a logical consequence of the spirit's disposition on the flesh, which is confirmed with the rigor of a law imposed by God Himself. Insofar as the spirit withdraws from the submission it owes to God, the flesh withdraws from the submission it owes to the spirit. Man finds punishment for his pride, which causes him to revolt against God, in the rebellion of his passions which rise up against reason and make him feel ashamed of himself. Fortunate is he when the resulting humiliation, through the direct action of grace which brings good out of evil, contributes to his return to God!

No other man was more just than St. Joseph or more humble in his justice, and no one will ever surpass or even equal him in chastity. The fact that he was chosen by God from the whole of humanity to become the Spouse of Mary, bears witness to a purity brighter than the sun.

Reflect upon this: St. Joseph's heart was created by God to love the most pure Virgin Mary. Hence, we can hold as certain that even though St. Joseph was conceived with original sin, by a special act of grace, no impure desire ever tainted his heart. God grants to certain saints an angelic favor: that concupiscence be extinguished in their flesh. We believe unquestioningly that Mary's future spouse enjoyed such a favor to an eminent degree. He was transported thereafter to the state St. Thomas Aquinas qualified as "the state of a purified soul" whereby earthly lusts are ignored.[1] In short, the chastity of St. Joseph was not a chastity of conflict and struggle, but a chastity which became part of his nature, very peaceful, as was necessary in order to be entitled to enter into marriage with Mary, the most holy Virgin.

Mary, likewise, found Joseph's heart in such perfect harmony with hers, that she entrusted herself to him, to remain a virgin in complete security.

God delighted in depicting an image of the chastity of St. Joseph in the person of the old

1. Cf. *Summa Theologica,* 1a 2æ, q. 61, a. 5, corpus.

Joseph, son of Jacob and Rebecca. This great patriarch had an innate horror of impure vice; he resisted the seduction of the wife of his master, the Egyptian Putiphar; he accepted being thrown into prison and being exposed to the most extreme torture for love of chastity.[2] This enlightened soul prefigures that of our Joseph.

The chastity of the old Joseph predisposed him to divine communication; he was instructed about the future through mysterious dreams.[3] Similarly, related St. Bernard, the new Joseph was made guardian of the celestial secrets of the angels, who were familiar at his bedside.[4]

O Saint, truly angelic and seraphic! O soul elevated above earthly concupiscence. O great saint, inspire all those who put their trust in you with chaste and celestial thoughts; obtain for all Christian spouses to unite only under holy intentions. With you, the flesh lived uniquely by the life of the spirit. How truly the lilies of virgins are secure in your hands! May the fragrance of these lilies, which embalm both the heavenly and the earthly Church, instill in us a desire for and love of purity! (Dom Bernard Maréchaux)

2. Cf. *Gen* 39:7-20
3. Cf. *Gen*, chapters 37, 40 and 41
4. Cf. *Mt* 1:20-21; 2:13; 2:20

The Freedom of Purity

A good nun, related Father de Barry, was tormented by violent and disturbing temptations, especially during prayer. She was so troubled that faintheartedness and mistrust took hold of her heart; she was convinced she would never attain that precious freedom of spirit that is here below the heavenly privilege of the children of God. Overwhelmed by anxiety, she had recourse to Mary as to her good Mother, to once and for all find peace and calm. “O Virgin!” she exclaimed, “if you feel that it is not for you to procure this grace for me, be so good then to at least direct me to those saints most dear to you, to a patron I can have recourse to with confidence and success.”

She had barely finished with her prayer, when her soul was flooded with consolation. St. Joseph appeared to her soul’s eyes as the saint who is dearest to the Virgin, as much in his capacity as spouse as for his outstanding virtues. Without any hesitation, she placed herself in the hands of this august protector, and instantly St. Joseph proved to her the efficacy of his intercession by delivering her soul from its distress. From then on, whenever and as soon as she felt attacked by the devil, she had recourse to the worthy Spouse of the Virgin Mary, and instantly she felt peace in her heart and freedom to converse sweetly with God.

The Bliss of Confession

A young girl took a vow of chastity. Having had the misfortune of being unfaithful, she could not find the courage to confess her sin. Beginning with the unworthy reception of the sacraments, she began a life full of remorse and torment. She was later inspired to have recourse to St. Joseph, and for nine days she devoutly recited the hymn and prayers to the saint. On completion of the novena, her feelings of shame disappeared, and—as she herself wrote in a letter to Father de Barry, asking him to make known this favor from St. Joseph—far from being painful, she found confession to be true bliss. "Convinced by this experience," she added, "of the power and the goodness of St. Joseph, I took with me his holy image with the resolution to never become separated from it, day or night. Since then, I have been able to overcome impure temptations and have received so many graces that I would not know how to acknowledge them all."

✠

Prayer to St. Joseph, Guardian of Virgins, to Obtain Purity

O St. Joseph, father and protector of virgins, to whose faithful care were entrusted Christ Jesus, Innocence itself, and Mary, the Virgin of virgins: I implore and beseech thee, through Jesus and Mary, these dearest treasures entrusted to thee, grant me that, preserved from all uncleanness, undefiled of mind, pure of heart and chaste of body, I may always serve Jesus and Mary in perfect chastity. Amen.

In honor of St. Joseph

Continually, and with docility, have recourse to St. Joseph, especially when tempted against purity.

EIGHTEENTH DAY

Humility and Virginity

Just as St. Joseph took care to guard his virtues under cover of a very holy humility, he was also diligent in hiding the precious pearl of his virginity. If he agreed to be married, it was so that, without anyone knowing it, he could hide his virtue under the veil of a holy marriage.

On this subject, virgins and those who wish to live in chastity, are taught that it is not sufficient to be celibate. If they are not humble and do not guard their purity in the precious vase of humility, they will be like the foolish virgins,[1] who, on account of their lack of humility and merciful charity, were turned down from the bridegroom's wedding feast and forced into the wedding feast of the world where the advice of our Divine Lord is not taken seriously. He says that you must be humble to have a share in the celebration, which means that it is necessary to practice humility, for

1. Cf. *Mt* 25:1-13.

He is the one who said: *When thou art invited to a wedding. . . . go and sit down in the lowest place.*[2]

Consequently we realize how necessary humility is in order to preserve virginity. It is well known that no one shall take part in the celestial banquet and the nuptial feast God prepares for virgins in His heavenly home, unless the person practices it. Precious things such as sweet-smelling ointments are not exposed to the open air, as the fragrance would gradually be lost in the environment and spoiled by insects. Likewise, holy souls, fearing to lose the value and merit of their good deeds, should place them for safe-keeping in a vessel, not in a common one, but in a precious alabaster vessel, like the one used by Mary Magdalene as she poured out the ointment over the sacred head of Our Lord.[3]

This alabaster vessel is the humility in which we must, in imitation of Our Lady and St. Joseph, keep our virtues and all that would draw admiration from the world, being happy to please the Lord and dwell under the sacred veil of self-abjection. We wait for God to come and take us to a safe place filled with His glory, and where He will Himself display our virtues for His honor and esteem.

. . . .

2. *Lk* 14:8,10.
3. Cf. *Mk* 14:3.

To what extent do we think St. Joseph possessed virginity, the virtue which renders us like angels, if the Most Blessed Virgin was not only completely pure and innocent, but virginity itself? How much do we think that the one who was called to be the guardian of her virginity, or better still, her companion (since she herself did not need to be protected by anyone) must have possessed this virtue!

Both had taken a vow of virginity for a lifetime when suddenly God asked them to be united in a holy wedding, not contrary to their wishes or retracting their vows, but rather reconfirming and strengthening them in their holy enterprise. Moreover, they vowed then to live their lives together in a virginal way. St. Joseph was not given to Our Lady in order to make her break her vow of virginity, but to be her companion, so that the chastity of Mary might be preserved in its entirety in a more wonderful way under the veil and the shade of their blessed marriage and of the holy union of life which they shared.

If the Blessed Virgin is a gate, said the Eternal Father, we wish it to remain shut because it is the east gate of the sanctuary that no one can enter or exit;[4] on the contrary, it has to be reinforced with incorruptible wood, meaning a companion who is pure and bears the name of St. Joseph, and who, therefore, has to surpass all the saints, even the

4. Cf. *Ez* 44:1-2.

angels and Cherubims, in this commendable virtue called virginity (St. Francis de Sales).

A Holy Card Conversion

A Christian mother had a daughter whose behavior was deplorable.

This afflicted mother never went into church without kneeling down in front of an image of St. Joseph, tearfully imploring the saint to obtain the conversion of her daughter.

One day she had an inspiration. "If I were to give her a picture of St. Joseph," she thought; and when her child was out, she went into her bedroom. On a table lay a book; and what a book!

"O St. Joseph," said the mother, "forgive me for putting your picture here, but I must!"

On her return, the girl resumed her reading.

"What is this?" she said. "A picture."

She turned it over and read automatically a prayer printed on the back.

God's grace awaited her there. She burst out crying and, filled with contrition, hurled the wicked book into the fire. She was converted.

The Marvels of Evening Prayer

In a humble house in Bordeaux, France, in the last century, lived a young woman whom people pitied with good reason for her sad and lonely life. Her husband, influenced by bad company, deserted the family home and only returned to curse its poverty and the privations awaiting him there.

His wife wept and prayed, but did not complain. To console her she had a young daughter whose angelic tenderness compensated for the loneliness caused by her husband's absence. In the evenings, during the long hours she spent alone, the poor mother taught her daughter prayers before she put her in the cradle. She would then lull her to sleep by repeating the sweet names of Jesus, Mary and Joseph.

One day, her husband, having failed to meet his pleasure-loving friends, decided to return home for the evening. As he was about to open the door, he stopped. He heard his wife's voice. "Whom can she be talking to?" he thought to himself, his heart already tormented by unjust suspicions. He gently pushed the door open. What a sight met his eyes! The young woman was on her knees with her daughter in her arms finishing her evening prayers. "Let us pray now, my dear child, for your father whom I love so much and whom I know you love, too. Let us commend him to St. Joseph, his patron saint." The little girl pressed her crossed hands more tightly to her chest and repeated this prayer with her mother. "O my God, O St. Joseph, bless him!"

Moved by this scene, the husband could not resist. He knelt down beside the cradle and prayed with his wife and beloved daughter. In response to his prayer God granted him love for his family and a purified heart. After that, as a good Christian and a happy father, he bid farewell to bad company and found his delight in family life.

✠

Prayer to St. Joseph, Model of Virtue

O Glorious St. Joseph, Spouse of the Immaculate Virgin, obtain for us pure, humble and charitable minds, and perfect resignation to the Divine Will. Be our guide, father and model through life, that we may merit to die as thou didst in the arms of Jesus and Mary. Amen.

St. Joseph, pray for us.

In honor of St. Joseph

Neglect none of the precautions necessary to safeguard the chastity of one's state so as to resemble St. Joseph.[5]

5. Cf. *Catechism of the Catholic Church*, n. 2520 and following.

NINETEENTH DAY

St. Joseph's Spirit of Silence

The prudence of St. Joseph had soared to the highest point possible, to the extent of seeing nothing but divine things, *sola divina intueatur.* It towered over the fleeting course of transitory things. We see him as a contemplative absorbed in God, as the man of silence and mystery who is on the earth without being of the earth and from whom nothing may, even for a moment, take away the thought of eternity.

Let us also admire him as a man of silence; to know how to refrain from speaking is an outstanding part of the virtue of prudence. Of a great talker Scripture says: *As a city that lieth open and is not compassed with walls, so is a man that cannot refrain his own spirit in speaking*[1]. . . . Joseph remains silent: he is a fortress preserving its hidden treasure behind impenetrable walls.

1. *Prov* 25:28.

Because the spirit of his silence was religious and prayerful, it became natural to him. The Gospel does not mention a single word spoken by him. It only tells us that he gave the Infant God the name of Jesus. . . . He said "Jesus" and no more. But in saying "Jesus," he said all—he said the word that enlightens all mysteries, the word on which humanity lives and shall live until the end of time. After him, let us all say again: "Jesus."

Not only did Joseph keep quiet, but nothing in his attitude revealed the secret of the Divinity of Jesus. His conduct made everyone believe he was the father of the adolescent growing up under his eyes. He acted this way without effort or restraint, through a high, instinctive-like prudence which guided all of his gestures with an overall sense of fidelity to the mission given him from Heaven.

Let us get to the bottom of this attitude of St. Joseph towards the Incarnate Word, and we shall then discover marvelous teachings. It is because of great virtue that faith and adoration grow with the familiarity of divine things. Too often, however, daily contact with things decreases respect. Joseph's familiarity in living with Jesus in no way diminished his adoration of the Son of God; on the contrary, it penetrated him even more keenly and led him to a complete and profound self-abasement. At the sight of humiliations encountered by the Divine Word, the humility of Joseph took on immeasurable proportions. Mankind has yet to know a greater and more humble worshipper of the Divine Majesty hidden under the veil of flesh than St. Joseph!

O, priests who consecrate the Eucharistic Body of Christ, O faithful who receive it, imitate the faith, respect, adoration and abundant love of this great saint in his dealings with the Word made flesh!

Let us all be inspired by his heavenly prudence so as to always act in conformity with the will of God. Let us obey the Holy Spirit, Sovereign Counselor of our soul, just as Joseph did. Let us conceal under a veil of silence the gifts received from Our Lord. Through the trials of this earthly life, let us fix our eyes on eternal goods, and let us try to aim all our efforts towards attaining them. This is the prudence of the saints (Dom Bernard Maréchaux).

A Worker of the Last Hour

Not so long ago an unhappy wretch, victim of his own dissoluteness and in dreadful poverty, was at the point of death. Charitable Christians, while trying to better his sad situation, had failed to convince him to accept any spiritual help.

In vain was he shown the everlasting misery towards which he was heading. His only response was a contemptuous sneer, truly diabolical. It was March, St. Joseph's month, and someone was inspired to turn to the great patriarch. On the 19th, prayers were intensified and St. Joseph was reminded that St. Teresa of Avila maintained that no one ever prayed to him in vain, especially on his feast day.[2] O the power of prayer! That happy day, the patient asked for spiritual help and requested someone to bring the priest he had slighted the most. He gathered what little strength he had left and made a full confession of his whole life with great contrition. A few hours later would have been too late. St. Joseph knew that. Before the end of the feast day of the glorious Spouse of Mary, this poor privileged penitent appeared before God, who in His infinite goodness wills to reward well the workers who come at the last hour.[3]

Glory and thanks to St. Joseph!

Reunited at Lunch

Several years ago in a religious house in Spain, on March 19th, the final day of a retreat for those who lived there, a cloud of sadness, caused by one of the gentlemen who persisted in an old quarrel with one of his companions, had dampened the general air of happiness.

But St. Joseph, to whom this unhappy matter had been entrusted, had prepared the best gift of the feast day.

At lunch time, Mr. N., laying aside his pride and resentment, approached the person with whom he was at odds moments before, and embraced him

---

2. Cf. First Day, p. 19.
3. Cf. *Mt* 20:9,12,14.

like a brother. Shedding tears of joy, they were reconciled in front of their companions, who were deeply moved and full of gratitude.

+

Iste, Quem Læti,

Hymn for Lauds on the Feast of St. Joseph
(Monastic Breviary)

He, whom the faithful joyously do honor,
Singing his praises with devout affection,
Won on this feast day, in eternal glory
Life everlasting.

Blest beyond others, and exceeding blissful,
For, when the moment of his death was nearing,
Jesus and Mary at his side were standing,
Soothing his spirit.

Death doth he conquer, laying down his burden,
Calmly he slumbers, rest he gains eternal;
Lo, round his forehead, bright with rays of splendor,
Shineth a garland.

Then, as he reigneth earnestly beseech we
That he may utter fervent intercessions,
Praying that pardon and the peace of Heaven
May be our portion.

Glory we give Thee, hymns of praise and blessing,
One in Three Persons, Who above art reigning,
God, Who hast honored with Thy crown forever
This Thy true servant. Amen.

Liturgical Prayer

(Collect from the Mass of St. Joseph, March 19th)

May we be helped, Lord, we pray, by the merits of the Spouse of Thy holy Mother, so that what we cannot obtain of ourselves, may be given to us through his intercession. Thou who art God, living and reigning with God the Father in the unity of the Holy Spirit, world without end. Amen.

In honor of St. Joseph

Never speak unnecessarily about oneself.

TWENTIETH DAY

Primacy of the Interior Life

The aura of silence that characterizes the behavior of St. Joseph extends also to his work as a carpenter in the house in Nazareth. However, it is silence which reveals in a special way his inner disposition. The Gospels speak exclusively of what Joseph "did"; but they allow, in his actions which are wrapped in silence, the discovery of an atmosphere of profound contemplation. Joseph was daily in contact with the mystery hidden for centuries, which made its dwelling under his roof. That explains, for example, why St. Teresa of Jesus, the great reformer of the contemplative Carmel, set herself to promote the renewal of the devotion given to St. Joseph in western Christianity.[1]

The complete sacrifice that Joseph made of his whole existence to the demands of the coming of the Messiah into his house finds its true motive in his unfathomable interior life, from which come to

1. Cf. First Day, pp. 17-20.

him special instructions and consolations, and whence flow for him the logic and the force, peculiar to simple and transparent souls, of great decisions—such as that by which he places immediately at the disposal of the divine plans his freedom, his lawful human profession, the happiness of his married life, and accepts the condition, the responsibility and the burdens of the family, renouncing the natural conjugal love which is its foundation and its food, for the benefit of a virginal love beyond compare.

This submission to God, which makes the will prompt to consecrate itself to all that concerns His service, is nothing but the exercise of the devotion that constitutes one of the expressions of the virtue of religion.[2]

The communion of life between Joseph and Jesus leads us to consider again the mystery of the Incarnation precisely under the aspect of the humanity of Christ, efficacious instrument of the divinity for the sanctification of souls. By virtue of the divinity, the human actions of Christ have been salutary for us, producing grace in us as much by reason of merit as by a certain efficacy.

Among these actions, the Evangelists give pride of place to those that concern the paschal mystery, but they do not fail to underline the importance of physical contact with Jesus in connection with cures[3]

---

2. Cf. St. Thomas, *Summa Theologica*, 2a 2æ, q. 82, a. 2.
3. Cf. for example, *Mk* 1:41.

and the influence that it exercised on John the Baptist when they were both in the womb of their mothers.[4]

The apostolic witness has not omitted to describe the birth of Jesus, the circumcision, the presentation in the temple, the flight into Egypt and the hidden life in Nazareth, by reason of the "mystery" of grace contained in such "deeds," all of which are salvific, because of their participation in the same source of love: the divinity of Christ. If this love, through His humanity, was shining on all men, the first of its beneficiaries were clearly those whom the divine will had placed in the closest intimacy with it: Mary, His Mother, and Joseph, His putative father.

Since the "fatherly" love of Joseph could not fail to influence the "filial" love of Jesus, and since, in turn, the "filial" love of Jesus could not fail to have its effect on the "paternal" love of Joseph, how are we to assess in depth this completely unique relationship? The souls that are most sensitive to the inspirations of divine love rightly see in Joseph a shining example of interior life.

Besides, the apparent tension between the active life and the contemplative life is transcended in him in an ideal way, as can happen in one who possesses the perfection of charity. According to the well-known distinction between the love of truth (*caritas veritatis*) and the requirement of love (*necessitas*

4. Cf. *Lk* 1:41-44.

caritatis), we can say that Joseph experienced just as much the *love of truth*, that is to say, the pure love of contemplating the divine truth which shone from the humanity of Christ, as the *requirement of love*, that is to say, the pure love of service required for the protection and the development of that same humanity (Pope John Paul II).

A Small Statue on a Big Truck

The street in front of the garden was so narrow that the big semitrailer loaded with steel beams for the framework of the chapel they were building could not find room to turn and enter the gate of the convent.

Not knowing what to do, the driver decided to go across an empty field and approach the site from the other side. Because of the heavy load the attempt was hazardous. In fact, after a few yards the truck got bogged up to its hubs in the loose soil still waterlogged from the recent rain. It was early afternoon. For four hours a team of workmen tried to disencumber the truck. At about six o'clock, having made no progress, they informed the Sisters who were quite unaware of the matter.

The Superior went to the spot, encouraged the men and concluded: "We must pray to St. Joseph." The workmen looked skeptical; the foreman let it be understood that he was not a Catholic. When the small statue of St. Joseph was brought, there was further astonishment. Brief explanations. . . . More skeptical smiles. "In any case," said an assistant, "it is not this statue that's going to get the truck out. It will only be done with plenty of hard work."

The good Mother did not answer. The efforts were resumed, with no other result than to make the heavy wheels spin in their muddy ruts. The beams which they slid under the vehicle gave way. The jacks, which proved useless, were cast aside. Discouraged, the workers wanted to leave and try again the next day.

Silently, the Mother Superior took the small statue of St. Joseph and tied it to the red cloth which was hanging from the longest beam of the load. Having done that, she asked them to try their luck once more. The foreman refused. "Come on," said the driver. "If we don't, Sister will try herself." He jumped to his seat and started the motor. The semitrailer shook, the wheels came out of the ruts, and two minutes later, the truck was on the road.

Silencing the exclamations of the crowd, the foreman went up to the Reverend Mother. "Thank you, Sister. It is really to St. Joseph that we owe this success."

+

Act of Consecration to St. Joseph

O Blessed St. Joseph! I consecrate myself to thy honor and give myself to thee, that thou mayest always be my father, my protector, and my guide in the way of salvation. Obtain for me a great purity of heart and a fervent love of the interior life. After thy example may I do all my actions for the greater glory of God, in union with the Divine Heart of Jesus and the Immaculate Heart of Mary! And do thou, O blessed St. Joseph, pray for me, that I may share in the peace and joy of thy holy death. Amen.

In honor of St. Joseph

Despite numerous occupations, consecrate every day at least twenty minutes to meditation on the Gospel or the writings of the saints, so as to be better aware of the Divine Will.

TWENTY-FIRST DAY

The Patience of St. Joseph

Appointed by God Himself to conceal and hide the ineffable mystery of the Incarnation, Joseph sheltered it under his humility and charity as beneath a veil of delicate linen of heavenly blue, scarlet and purple;[1] then, so as to shield it from all inclemencies, he covered it again with the impermeable cloak of his infinite patience.

In admiring the patience of this great saint, the Church, calling it a mirror, invites us to contemplate in it the greatness of his virtue.

To be patient is to bear, without complaining or being discouraged, the evils that press upon us, no matter how prolonged they may be: adversities arising from circumstances, from unjust behavior or ill-treatment by others, the attacks both interior and exterior of evil spirits, and even the apparent rejection from God who, as Job tells us, is pleased to train his servants to the point of tormenting

1. Cf. *Ex* 26:31.

them in an extraordinary way: *Mirabiliter me crucias—Thou tormentest me wonderfully.*[2]

To be patient, says St. Thomas Aquinas, is also to react victoriously against the sadness which arises from the actual pressure of evil, and to maintain throughout a holy joy within one's heart.[3]

How patient St. Joseph was from this double point of view! We know nothing of what he suffered in Nazareth, or in the land of Egypt, which was an exile for him; but we are certain that he suffered a great deal, both through the privations of his exile, and through the activities of men and of demons. Then there was his constant concern to take upon himself all the sorrows and distresses, and to let nothing get so far as to affect either Mary or Jesus. His patience was a shield which received and blunted all hostile deeds; his vocation, his happiness consisted in sacrificing himself daily for the benefit of Jesus and Mary.

In seeing St. Joseph toiling as a workman at his task and suffering as one oppressed, it was not easy to realize the eminence of his virtue—no more than the treasures hidden by his humble and laborious life; one did not know that the soul of this poor workman was full of radiance and ecstasies, and that his home was a foretaste of Heaven.

Let us acclaim the patience of this great saint, and imitate it so far as it is within our power.

2. *Job* 10:16.

3. Cf. *Summa Theologica*, 1a 2æ, q. 66, a. 4, ad 2; and also 2a 2æ, q. 128, corpus.

Today, freed from the obscurity of the present life, it shines with a wonderful brilliance; it demands the special praise decreed for it by the Church.

St. James informs us that patience gives to good works the final mark of perfection.[4] It is certain that the devil tries by all possible means to weary and to tire the patience of God's servants, so that they let go and do not pursue to the end the work for which God has placed them in a certain place, in a certain combination of circumstances. It is up to them, aware of the divine will, to keep their courage beyond defeat through trust, and to hold on without weakening.

Be patient, St. James urges, *until the coming of the Lord. . . . which is at hand.*[5] So the duration of patience is that of human life; but that is so short! And each day brings us closer to the coming of the Lord. So let us be patient. For his part, St. Paul says that *tribulation worketh patience; and patience trial; and trial hope*; *and*, he adds, *hope confoundeth not.*[6] So patience strengthens hope, and that in turn supports patience in showing it the crown that is assured.

Ah! how deep a look St. Joseph cast on the brevity of this life! And what boundless hope arose in his heart! But had he to suffer without respite and without end for Jesus and Mary, he would have accepted suffering on those terms. To suffer through love of those so lovable, that was his very

4. Cf. *James* 1:2-4. 5. *Ibid.* 5:7-8. 6. *Rom* 5:3-5.

life, that was his happiness (Dom Bernard Maréchaux).

St. Joseph's Bird

In one house of the Little Sisters of the Poor in Montreal there was a canary whose songs cheered the hearts of the old folk. One day, however, "Beauty" caught a cold and died. Looking at the empty bird-cage, the patients voiced their concern: "We will all get bored to tears, we must get another bird!"—"Fair enough, ask St. Joseph for one!"

An old artist sketched an outline of the bird they wanted, with notes cascading from its half-open beak, and wrote above the drawing, "Good St. Joseph, send us a song-bird quickly!" Prayers were joined to the request, and it was very clear that the old people were entirely confident of a favorable reply.

One warm, sunny morning, when the windows were wide open, a pretty, little, white bird came and landed on the table of one of the patients who missed "Beauty" very greatly. He welcomed the visitor with joy, and offered it some of his lunch, which the bird accepted with alacrity. Very soon, by mutual agreement, bird and patient were eating off the same dish. A postulant Little Sister arrived on the scene just in time to enjoy this charming sight; she tried to grab the bold guest, but it took wing through the same window through which it had entered. A few moments later it returned—perhaps to finish its rudely interrupted meal—but this time the postulant was more deft, and soon the cage was adorned with the most gracious of prisoners. "It's St. Joseph's bird," the old folk said, whenever they told its story to visitors. And from far and near, people came to see "St. Joseph's bird."

Free Apples

In a home of the Little Sisters of the Poor, "Sister Cook" was short of apples which were rare and expensive that year. In a confident gesture, she set an apple at the foot of a statue of St. Joseph. A few days later, another home of theirs received a telephone call notifying them that a truckful of apples had accidentally overturned on the road, and their help in picking up the apples would be appreciated. . . . Thus, they inherited a truckload of apples!

+

The *Memorare* to St. Joseph

(Composed by Pope Pius IX)

Remember, O most chaste Spouse of the Virgin Mary, that never has it been known
that anyone who asked for thy help and sought thy intercession was left unaided.
Full of confidence in thy power,
I hasten to thee, and beg thy protection.

Listen, O foster-father of the Redeemer,
to my humble prayer,
and in thy goodness hear and answer me. Amen.

In honor of St. Joseph

Resolve never to grumble against Divine Providence, especially when in the midst of great difficulties.

TWENTY-SECOND DAY

Lover of Poverty

The great St. Joseph knew poverty, even destitution. He was forced to live from day to day on his labor; he had to seek work under difficult and humiliating conditions, waiting oftentimes with great worry, and despite his assiduous labor and the privations he imposed on himself, he was not always able to shield Mary and Jesus from the discomfort of poverty.

He was poor, but he loved poverty; he never wished to replace it with the treasures and the oriental luxury of his forefather, King Solomon. If Moses preferred the harsh and persecuted life of his Hebrew brothers—which prophetically depicted the shame of Christ to come—to all the opulence and delights of the corrupted Egyptian court, St. Joseph himself, and even more so than Moses, enlightened by the Holy Spirit, respected and embraced poverty as a priceless treasure.

The goods of the world are in opposition to the goods of Heaven; holy souls do not wish to have riches unless it be to distribute them among the poor. They cannot resign themselves to supine enjoyment of the comforts of life when there are so many humans who do not even have the basic necessities.

The Son of God, coming into this world, could have made use of the goods of this world without fear that His thrice-holy soul might be contaminated by their use, but He wished to banish them from His human life and have no experience of them whatsoever. He was born poor, poor He lived, and poor He died. Between the manger of His birth and the gibbet of His last breath, poverty occupied every instant of His human existence. He thereby gave us the example we needed to hold worldly goods in contempt; and even more, it was His adorable charity which impelled Him to take His place among the poor and the disinherited. Having taken upon Himself the cloak of poverty, He rendered it lovable and full of victorious attractions. He impressed by anticipation into the souls of Mary, His Mother, and Joseph, His adopted father, the love of poverty, which, since His coming, has led so many souls after Him.

St. Joseph delighted in taking a poor wife, Mary; and Mary was delighted to take a poor husband, Joseph. O holy union of two souls, both poor and virgins, in whom were manifested incomparable riches, from which proceeded an affection purer than light itself. If there were ever two spouses who loved each other in a chaste manner and in God, without any regard for the advantages of the world, they were Mary and Joseph.

This poverty, which was one of the distinctive signs of his union with Mary, was precious to St. Joseph. He felt its thorns during the flight into Egypt, and he felt its bruises under the humble roof in Nazareth. But he loved these thorns and bruises; the thorns blossomed and the bruises turned into joys.

Nothing can compare with the charm of the cradle of the religious orders, because the poverty of Bethlehem and Nazareth are usually found there initially. Later on comforts are introduced; the religious are well-housed, well-fed, and want for nothing, but the joy of serving God wanes, and the purity of vocations leaves much to be desired. It is for this reason that God allows catastrophes which suddenly bring the orders back to primitive poverty.

O St. Joseph, spread the love for poverty throughout the Church and the souls of men. You are the foster-father of the poor; the poverty you lived under with Jesus and Mary was so great, but you provided for their needs; you will not fail to provide for those religious families who truly love poverty, and it is especially in their favor that your providence is so admirably displayed.

Protect also all the poor, those for whom poverty is a way of life, a necessity; teach them to make it holy by resignation, to soften it by perfect confidence in God, and to arrive at a sincere contempt for worldly goods, for it is by the contempt for worldly goods that one reaches heavenly riches (Dom Bernard Maréchaux).

Babushka, Michail and the Faith

This scene took place in Russia, in a house where all signs of religion had disappeared. Only the Babushka (the grandmother) in the upper room had remained faithful to Christ.

One day, she took from her hiding-place the icon of St. Joseph and lit two candles, when Michail, her grandson, surprised her in prayer. The child asked her a thousand questions and expressed interest in all that she told him.

He could not wait to tell his mother that he had prayed to St. Joseph with Babushka. Matryona, a fierce atheist, reacted like a wounded viper. "Little fool, you repeat what old women say. In Russia, there is no longer a Good God; there are no longer saints nor any St. Joseph." Then in a more calm tone, "Tell me, Michail, have you already seen the Good God? Have you ever met St. Joseph? Has the Infant Jesus ever given you anything? Dear Child, those are stories which uneducated old ladies believe. Woe to you if you put faith in what Grandma says. The soldiers will come and take us all as they took Uncle Ivan. Then you will call on God in vain. He won't be interested in our fate; is that understood?"

Yelissei, the father, watched the scene with inner disquiet. The sound of troika bells brought him back to reality. Some friends from Matryona's home country had invited themselves to stay for several days. They were welcomed with proverbial Russian hospitality. Life in this isolated place would be less monotonous. Thanks to the splendid troika, they organized long trips, and the days passed quickly. Then came the feast of St. Joseph, which used to be celebrated with solemnity to the sound of bells.

In the absence of the family and of their guests, Babushka lit some candles before the icon of St. Joseph and prayed to this great saint in union with many Russian hearts that had remained faithful to the faith of their fathers.

The following day Matryona returned with the child, who was ill. In the evening, all of his limbs were shivering. The fever increased, and the parents were distraught. The visitors left and promised to send a doctor from the nearest village. The mother watched at his bedside day and night. When at last the doctor arrived, he could only shake his head and declare the child to be lost. He offered to stay with them, if they wished, until the final and fatal moment. The father accepted this kind offer and they hoped against all hope. As for Matryona, who was desperate, she went up to her mother-in-law and begged her to light the candles. "I wish to pray with you, Babushka," she said. "Michail has only a few hours to live. If he recovers, I will believe and never mock again." She burst into tears and repeated the prayers recited by the old woman. Then, going down again to her little boy and never taking her eyes off of him, she waited, moving her lips as in prayer.

The sick child was delirious and could have died at any moment; but this was not to be. After midnight, Michail became more calm and, little by little, he went off to sleep. At the same time the fever came down. Reassured, the doctor rose and said, "There is nothing more for me to do here. The Devil must have intervened; I cannot explain it otherwise. Good-bye. Be happy!"

Matryona followed the doctor with a detached, lost look. Yelissei did not understand the behavior of his wife, who said to him, "My dear Yelissei, I don't know what to say. Go to Mama and she will explain everything to you." Sobbing, she threw herself on her knees and murmured, "My God, I believe. . . . St. Joseph, I thank you."

After learning what had happened, Yelissei knelt close to his wife and they prayed together. Then he kissed her and went to seek his mother, whose fidelity to the faith had brought about this miracle and the happiness of the family.

The following morning, Michail opened his eyes and looked at his parents in astonishment, then asked for something to eat. His convalescence filled his parents with joy; but even greater was the joy of having once again found the faith.

✠

Ave Joseph

Ave, Joseph, fili David, sponse castissime gloriosæ Virginis Mariæ, Domini nostri Jesu Christi educator optime.

Pie sancte Joseph, ora pro nobis pueris tuis; ora pro parvula nostra familia quam sub tua tutela potentissimoque tuo præsidio accipere dignatus es.

Hail, Joseph, son of David, most chaste Spouse of the glorious Virgin Mary, perfect educator of Our Lord Jesus Christ.

Good St. Joseph, pray for us, thy children; pray for our little family which thou hast deigned to take under the care of thy most powerful protection. Amen.[1]

In honor of St. Joseph

Endure all daily frustrations for love of God, as an occasion to practice spiritual poverty. Poverty should not frighten the true children of St. Joseph.

1. Cf. another version of this prayer on Second Day, p. 31.

TWENTY-THIRD DAY

Obedience of Jesus to St. Joseph

The very example of Jesus Christ, who, on earth, wished to give proof of such great respect and obedience towards St. Joseph, should be sufficient to move us all to become fervently devoted to this great saint.

Jesus, from the very instant His Heavenly Father assigned Joseph to take His place on earth, always regarded him as His father, and therefore showed him respect and obedience for thirty years: *Et erat subditus illis—And He was subject to them*;[1] which means that during all this time, the sole occupation of the Redeemer was to obey Mary and Joseph.

During all this time, it was for Joseph to give orders as he was established head of this little family, and it was for Jesus to obey as a subordinate, to the extent that He never undertook any action, not even a small step, nor ever ate His food,

1. *Lk* 2:51.

nor went to sleep except by the orders of St. Joseph. . . .

This humble obedience of Jesus shows that the dignity of Joseph is superior to that of all the saints, except that of the Divine Mother.

Thus, it is with reason that a learned writer said, "He is worthy of being honored by men, whom the King of Kings wished to elevate to such heights." Also Jesus Christ Himself recommended to St. Margaret of Cortona "to have a special devotion to St. Joseph as the one who nourished Him during His life" (St. Alphonsus de Liguori).

★

★ ★

"Joseph not only had the name of father of Jesus, but he also had the reality of it, as much as any man could," said St. John Damascene.

It is not the begetting alone which constitutes paternity, but also the authority and cares of government. . . . Is there any function of the best of fathers which was not gloriously executed by this faithful and prudent servant, whom the Lord chose to govern His family? Was it not Joseph who received the Child Jesus and placed Him on the manger's straw? Was it not Joseph who reddened the circumcision knife with the Most Precious Blood when he circumcised Jesus? We know in fact that it was the father who was chosen to perform this sacrament on his children. Was it not Joseph who saved Him from the furies of Herod, His persecutor? Was it not he who supplied Him with food, clothing and lodging, during thirty years, from the labor of his hands and the sweat of his brow?

How many times did the arms of St. Joseph serve as a cradle for the Child Jesus! What tender kisses he lavished upon Him! How often did he feed Him with his hands, dress Him, teach Him to speak and to work! How many times, when this Divine Child had grown up, did Joseph rest on His Heart!

If Joseph was such a tender father to Jesus, what was Jesus to Joseph? No doubt that He was for him the best of sons, that He was submissive, obedient and respectful in all things, as He was towards His Father (St. Leonard of Port-Maurice).

St. Joseph Addressing the Divine Child Jesus *(St. Alphonsus de Liguori)*

Since Thou the name of father hast bestowed
On me, my Jesus, let me call Thee Son.
My Son! I love—I love Thee; yes, my God!
Forever will I love Thee, dearest One!

Thou art my God! I humbly Thee adore;
But, as my Son, ah! bid me kiss Thy face,
And make my heart remain for evermore
Close bound with sweetest chains in Thy embrace!

Since Thou hast deigned to choose me here below
The nurse and guardian of Thy life to be,
My sweetest Love! my Good! ah! let me know
What willest Thou?—what does Thou ask of me?

All, all I am, to Thee I now resign;
My love I consecrate to Thee alone;
And know, my heart is mine no more—'Tis Thine;
My very life I do not call my own.

Since Thou art pleased to share my humble home,
And be on earth companion of my love,
Well may I hope, dear Jesus, to become
Thy loved companion in Thy home above.

"One Hundred, Not One Less!"

St. Joseph's Orphanage, on Great Slave Lake in Canada, was threatened by an imminent famine in March of 1917. One hundred orphans, ten nuns and as many fathers and brothers felt the gnawing pangs of hunger. They dared not think of caribou, for the hunters up to five hundred kilometers away said that the woods favored by these reindeer for their wintering were deserted. The brothers caught only four trout in eight days with their seventy fishing poles stretched out together over a long distance in the deep water under the ice.

One night, Father Duport, superior of the mission, utterly consumed with worry, went to the dining-hall where he found the children seated at the table around small roasted pieces of the last fish. Assuming a dissatisfied air, he said:

"My children, if we are destitute, it is not the fault of our brothers, nor of the sisters, for they have tried everything, and have sacrificed all for you. It's your fault!"

Several children, believing they were being reproached for having eaten too much, began to sob.

"That is not the reason," continued the Father Superior. "If I am angry, very angry, it is because you are not praying to St. Joseph with enough fervor. That is what I wanted to tell you."

Upon this explanation, all the little ones stood up and promised to pray "with all their might."

The superior, asked to determine the number of caribou necessary to save the mission, responded that they needed "one hundred, not one less."

"Well, my children, on your knees!"

A new novena began, to call upon St. Joseph to provide the one hundred necessary caribou.

Father Duport sent for the two hired hunters of the mission.

"Prepare your dogs immediately and leave."

The hunters shrugged their shoulders: "But you know as well as we do, Father, that there are no more. It's impossible."

"Leave," replied the Father, "go and kill one hundred caribou, not one less. St. Joseph owes them to us, because we need them and we asked him for them. He will send them to us."

Feeling quite sure they were going to fail, but paid for it anyway, the two men left.

They had not walked two days, a short distance for that country, when a countless army of reindeer stood before them, coming from the east, against all known habits, in Indian memory, of these nomadic animals.

Dumbfounded to see so suddenly and in this place, more caribou than they had ever seen together at one time, the hunters gathered their senses, took position and shot at the herd which ran away at top speed. A reindeer fell, sometimes two, with each shot of their powerful rifles. When the herd broke up, the Indians counted the dead. There were one hundred and three.

It was at the precise moment that the sisters and the orphans, united at the chapel for the novena, implored St. Joseph in a heart-rending prayer to quickly supply the one hundred caribou, not one less.

+

Prayer to St. Joseph for All Spiritual Blessings

O St. Joseph, whose protection is so great, so strong, so prompt before the throne of God, I place in thee all my interests and desires. O, St. Joseph, do assist me by thy powerful intercession, and obtain for me from thy Divine Son, Jesus Christ Our Lord, all spiritual blessings, so that, having engaged here below thy heavenly power, I may offer my thanksgiving and homage to the most loving of fathers. O, St. Joseph, I never weary contemplating thee and Jesus asleep in thy arms; I dare not approach while He reposes near thy heart. Press Him in my name and kiss His fine head for me; and ask Him to return the kiss when I draw my dying breath. St. Joseph, patron of departing souls, pray for me. Amen.

In honor of St. Joseph

Obey one's superiors in all that is not sinful, following the example of St. Joseph, as if God Himself were commanding it.

TWENTY-FOURTH DAY

The Director of Wisdom Incarnate

"Is He not the son of that carpenter?"[1] is what the Jews were asking about Jesus. Yes, answers St. Peter Chrysologus, indeed He is the Son of a Carpenter, but what kind of carpenter? In fact He is the Son of Him who made the world, not by means of a hammer but by a decree of His will; He it was who devised the elements, not by a mere stroke of genius but by a simple command. He it was who illuminated the sun not with an earthly fire but by a superior heat. In fact He was the Son of an Artisan whose Word created everything out of nothing.

You are right, holy Doctor of the Church, for Jesus is truly the Son of the great Workman who made the universe. To the glory of Joseph, one may also say that Jesus is the Son of that poor carpenter who handles the saw and the plane. It was the Blessed Virgin herself who gave to Joseph this

---

1. Cf. *Mt* 13:55.

beautiful title: the father of Jesus;[2] so let us therefore say with confidence that Jesus is the Son of that humble carpenter and in this very capacity submitted Himself to him, being at the same time a companion to his toils. O, what a marvel just to imagine this!

Jesus helped St. Joseph to work with wood, as He molded the world together with the Eternal Father. O, most wonderful dignity of Joseph! exclaims Gerson. Sublime grandeur that makes us see Joseph as an emulator of God Himself. A poor carpenter working with wood, emulator of One who created the world! What more do you need to proclaim Joseph the greatest of all men as a father, since God Himself cannot make a father greater than the one who has God for a Son?

There are three things, says the Angelic Doctor, which are so awesome that even God Himself cannot make anything greater: the humanity of Our Lord Jesus Christ, cause of its hypostatic union with the Word; the glory of the elect, whose principal object is God's infinite being; and the Mother of God, who has no equal and of whom it has been said: "Majorem quam Matrem Dei non potest facere Deus: Greater than the Mother of God, God could not make." God could not do greater honor to a person than to make her His very own Mother.

2. Cf. *Lk* 2:48.

Let us repeat, to the glory of Joseph, that God cannot make a father greater than the one who has God for his Son (St. Leonard of Port-Maurice).

A Protestant Lady and the Master of the House

In the middle of March in the year 1867, a paralytic woman of Protestant denomination was brought into a Canadian nursing home which was under the patronage of St. Joseph. She came there to find a cure for her suffering and had no intention of changing her religion. She even explained it to one of her friends, saying: "It'll take somebody really smart to catch me." She was not acquainted with St. Joseph, even less did she know of his skills for winning a soul for God.

Each day, the Sisters working in the nursing home made the devotions for the month of March and addressed their prayers to St. Joseph for the poor paralytic. Without her knowing, they sewed into the folds of her dress two medals, one of the Blessed Virgin Mary, the other of St. Joseph. One day a Sister brought St. Joseph into her conversation with the sick lady. "St. Joseph?" replied the Protestant lady, "I don't know the man; I have never seen him."

"How is that?" answered the Sister. "You are in a house whose master you do not know?"

And, opening her prayer book, she handed her a picture of St. Joseph. "My! How good looking he is!" she said as she studied the picture.

The good Sister described St. Joseph to the sick lady the best way she could. To her great surprise the lady took the picture, kissed it with respect and asked to keep it. From that day on she had no other consolation than to hear St. Joseph spoken of, to have his life and virtues described to her. She had a young son whom pious friends introduced to the Catholic faith. He went to his mother to ask her to let him make his profession of faith, which was arranged for the first of May; she agreed to this wholeheartedly. Scarcely had he left her when she sent for the house chaplain: "Sir," she said, "I wish to become a Catholic. I want to be baptized at the same time as my son! Please be so kind as to instruct me in the faith."

She was instructed and prepared, so that on the first of May the mother and the son could be seen at the foot of St. Joseph's altar, mingling their tears with the holy water which flowed down from their foreheads. On the last day of the same month, the new Catholics made their First Holy Communion and received the Sacrament of Confirmation together.

Happy are they who know St. Joseph well and make him known to others!

✠

Liturgical Prayer

(Collect from the Mass of St. Joseph the Worker, May 1st)

O God, the Creator of all things, Thou dost impose on man the law of work; grant in Thy goodness that, by the example of St. Joseph and under his patronage, we may accomplish the work that Thou dost command us to do and attain the reward that Thou hast promised us. Through Our Lord Jesus Christ, Thy Son, who liveth and reigneth with Thee in the unity of the Holy Spirit, One God, world without end. Amen.

In honor of St. Joseph

Make it a daily habit to do a good deed: make a little sacrifice to deliberately mortify the sense of taste; renounce a personal preference in order to be agreeable to one's neighbor; have concern for those in difficulty; pray for the sick, the dying, the souls in Purgatory.

TWENTY-FIFTH DAY

Model of Workers

Out of what beneficent goodness did Providence give St. Joseph as a model to workers! St. Joseph was a craftsman. Jesus Himself was, too, and under the eyes of His adopted father, so good was He at His craft that He was usually called the son of the carpenter, the son of the worker.[1]

What a lesson of humility for human pride! The Son of God came down to earth to be an example to man and at the same time to pour His grace upon him, which grace was contained in His examples. The human actions of Jesus are not simple gestures that we are to imitate—they are, in addition, reservoirs of inexhaustible, superabundant graces for humanity, and from which one can draw limitlessly.

It was necessary that the actions of the Son of God be imitable by all men; that is why it pleased

1. Cf. *Mt* 13:55; *Mk* 6:3.

Him to choose for Himself and for His earthly family a life most humble, that of an artisan. In adopting this life for Himself and His own, He sanctified it for all those who lead such a life and provided living springs of grace which are available to the humblest and the littlest of all.

Now Jesus, in His wisdom and gentle Providence, decided to entrust very specially into the hands of St. Joseph, His adopted father, under whose eyes He was apprenticed as a worker, all the graces that He acquired in those thirty years with him. This he did in order to be able to pour them out on the immense multitude of human beings for whom the necessity of earning daily bread consists in leaning over a worker's bench or an artisan's table.

Joseph the worker is the model and patron of workers; he it is who dispenses the graces of Jesus the Worker. To these graces Joseph adds the precious contribution of his own merits.

When a worker is faithful to God, St. Joseph scatters choice blessings on him and his family. It is not rare for God to draw from these blessings saintly preachers, rescuers of souls, just as he drew Jesus, the Saviour of the world, from the workshop of St. Joseph.

O! would that contemporary society, disillusioned with sophisms and fallacious promises, recognize that nowhere is the worker's humble life so much honored as it is in the Church! The Church could not underestimate it without doing a disservice to its origin, because it emerged from the house of Nazareth where Joseph, Mary and Jesus lived by the work of their hands.

O, St. Joseph, raise up apostles from those working in the world and lead them back to God under the noble patronage of your example.

Let us recognize here a commendable design of Providence. The life of Joseph the worker was a humble life, and because of this, it was doomed to be forgotten. Here is precisely how, from this life of humility, God could fashion a patronage that extends itself to billions of human beings and, one may even say, to all humanity that is subject to the law of work. Far above the half-faded images of founders of empires, law-givers and conquerors, appears the gentle and inspired face of St. Joseph the Worker, brightened by the divine radiance of Jesus. That is how God glorifies the humble! (Dom Bernard Maréchaux).

Miraculous Staircase in Santa Fe

In 1873, the Sisters of the Academy of Our Lady of Light of Loretto, in Santa Fe, New Mexico, in the southwest part of the United States of America, engaged Mexican carpenters to construct a gothic chapel modelled upon the Sainte-Chapelle of Paris. Conceived by the architect Mouly, this structure was built in five years at the cost of $30,000. It measured 22.50 meters (74 feet) in length, 7.50 meters (25 feet) in width and 25.50 meters (84 feet) in height.

The structure was almost completed when an error or an omission was noticed: there was no means to ascend to the choir loft which was at the back of the chapel. Several carpenters were called to the scene, but they all answered the same: on account of the height of the loft, it was impossible to build a staircase; the stairs would take up too much space in the nave. As a result, it would become necessary to make use of a ladder, or completely rebuild the loft.

In great consternation the Sisters decided to entrust to St. Joseph, whose feast day was drawing near, this humanly insoluble dilemma. They began a novena in his honor.

On the last day of the novena, a gray-haired man leading a donkey and carrying a tool chest stopped at the Academy. He asked to speak with Mother Magdalene, the superior in charge of the convent at that time, and offered to build the stairs. Delighted, Mother Magdalene accepted his offer immediately.

The construction of the stairs lasted about six months. Certain Sisters who were present at the work site remarked that the mysterious worker had used only a saw, a T-square and a hammer. They remembered seeing tubs of water filled with pieces of soaking wood. When Mother Magdalene looked for the worker to pay him, he was nowhere to be found. A reward was offered; no one claimed it. Even the local lumber yard gave no proof of purchase for the wood used.

The completed work is a circular staircase of thirty-three steps consisting of two complete spirals, at 360°, without any central support. It rests above against the loft and below on the floor, where the entire weight seems to be supported. Woodpegs take the place of nails.

During the course of the years, architects and builders from numerous foreign countries have inspected this architectural wonder. They all marvel to see how the stairs still remain standing.

Certain people thought that it would fall apart as soon as it was used, but, in spite of daily use, the staircase remains in place even after more than a century.

At the Academy, Sister Mary, then thirteen years old, was one of the first to mount these stairs with her friends. However, being frightened, they came down on their hands and knees. We can easily understand how, having no railing for support, they were afraid.

Several experts in building materials affirm that the curved stringers had been installed with precision. The wood is spliced in seven different places on the inside and in nine different places on the outside, with each piece forming a perfect curve. Moreover, this wood is of a hard variety and is not native to New Mexico. Its origin is still a mystery.

In connection with the redesign of the main electrical service and meter loop for the building,

Mr. Carl Albach had to climb the stairway a number of times. Each time he went up or came down, he seemed to feel a small amount of vertical movement, as if the two 360° turns were taken out of a large coiled spring. He was not the only one to have experienced this phenomenon. Mother Ludavine also had the same experience in ascending the stairs. Perhaps in this very phenomenon lies the secret of its construction.

Is St. Joseph himself the builder of this magnificent miraculous staircase? Be that as it may, the Sisters of the Academy of Loretto are certain that the stairs were the response to their confident prayers to St. Joseph, the glorious Spouse of Our Lady, the model of workers and the consoler of the afflicted.

✠

Prayer of Pope St. Pius X to St. Joseph, Model of Workers

Glorious St. Joseph, model of all who are devoted to work, obtain for me the grace to work in a spirit of penance, in order thereby to atone for my many sins; to work conscientiously, putting devotion to duty before my own inclinations; to labor with gratitude and joy, deeming it an honor to employ and to develop, by my labor, the gifts I have received from Almighty God; to work with order, peace, moderation, and patience, without ever shrinking from weariness and difficulties; to work above all with a pure intention and with self-detachment, having always before my eyes the hour of death and the accounting which I must then render of time wasted, of talents unemployed, of good undone, and of my empty pride in success, which is so prejudicial to the work of God.

All for Jesus, all through Mary, all in imitation of thee, O Patriarch Joseph! This shall be my motto in life and in death. Amen.

In honor of St. Joseph

Throughout each day's work, offer all for Jesus, all through Mary, all in imitation of St. Joseph: let this be our motto in life and in death.

TWENTY-SIXTH DAY

Model of Sanctity in Family Life

Families who wish to be Christian should resort to the patronage of St. Joseph. In this they will receive very special help in order to realize their noble ideal.

"Joseph leads us directly to Mary, and Mary leads us to the source of all holiness, to Jesus who has consecrated family virtues by His own submission to Joseph and Mary. Thus our desire is to see all Christian families renewed by modeling themselves upon such beautiful examples of virtue. In this way, when the human community rests upon the foundation of the family, the day that the domestic social unit shall acquire more stability, when conjugal sanctity,[1] harmony and fidelity shall be safeguarded more religiously, at that very instant shall be seen a new kinship, like a new force, spread across all the members of the human society, and the virtue of Christ penetrate into its very depths.

1. Which in no way allows for contraception or abortion.

That day we shall see flower not only the reform of personal morals, but also the reform of social and national life" (Pope Benedict XV).

These are words to meditate on. They reveal to us the secret of the intercession and the influence of St. Joseph. He works together with Mary and Jesus. He has his very own powerful influence, but he is likewise the mediator of the incomparable flow of graces which emanate from Mary his Spouse, and of the graces which flow from the source of all graces, Jesus, his adopted Son.

If he is invoked as the noble head of the Holy Family, he acts in this capacity. His action is, so to speak, reinforced by Mary's and carries with it the all-powerful action of Jesus. Such is the union of three persons within the Holy Family, that it would be impossible to separate their manner of operating. Joseph, as the head, represents the Family in its entirety, and from this position his intervention seems decisive to us.

Let us address ourselves to him with confidence so that he may heal the evils and disastrous lesions which disfigure the contemporary family, that he may make the impious law of divorce return to the depths of hell from whence it was ejected, that he may also correct and make disappear from the souls of spouses the latent separation of wills and contradictory tendencies which make the good upbringing of children impossible, that he may give back to spouses the sentiment of their dignity as procreators.

O St. Joseph, grant that under the married roof spouses may be united, *unanimes in domo*,[2] one in faith, one in the love of God and in attachment to His holy will, so that the family may be a seed-bed of Christians and of the elect.

It is a question of rendering a Christian sense of things to souls, which will make them enter into the true meaning of the present life, a life of labor and of trial, not of enjoyment, but also a life of hope and of merit. By this are lusts extinguished, worries calmed. Souls, accepting the order willed by God, walk in a peace which nothing can trouble and which spills over onto society. Doubtless this infusion of Christian meaning constitutes a great miracle of grace. Let us pray with confidence for St. Joseph to make it come about. It is not beyond his power.

It is to St. Joseph then that we must have recourse, the minister of the counsels of the Most High, who has been proclaimed the Protector of the Universal Church (Dom Bernard Maréchaux).

Family Reconciled

A devout servant of St. Joseph recently wrote these touching words:

"St. Joseph has just granted a special favor to our family. At the time of my mother's death, a

2. *Ps* 67:7.

distressing event brought our family trouble and dissension. One of my sisters found herself not only wronged but dishonored. After a violent argument, all ties were broken, and the two parties no longer wished to see or speak to one another. Both sides said repeatedly that any attempt at reconciliation would be useless. And in fact, all attempts in this direction proved fruitless. With a broken heart I appealed to St. Joseph. 'You are the advocate of hopeless cases,' I said. 'If you grant my request, I promise, for a whole year, to pay a visit each day to your statue at the end of the garden and make known publicly the grace you granted me.'

"St. Joseph made me wait, but I never stopped pestering him about it. Everyone told me to resign myself to my cross, since all hope seemed lost. I decided to make a last effort. I wrote to my sister and her husband, quoting the words of Our Lord in the Gospel about the forgiveness of insults and the love of enemies. I then went and placed my letter at the foot of our good St. Joseph, beseeching him to bless it, to accompany it and to soften their hearts.

"O the wonderful goodness of this great saint! My sister and her husband, who until then had resisted every attempt at reconciliation, were won over. They went to meet the person who had insulted them.

"This very person, because of her age, her social standing, etc., should have been the one to take the first step.

"She was dumbfounded when my brother-in-law called on her, very gently asked her to read my letter, then extended his hand, assuring her that what was past was past, and that he desired nothing but the re-establishment of close family ties. They embraced each other tenderly and, from that moment on, everything changed. All animosity disappeared, no negative thoughts nor guilty feelings remained.

"The following Sunday, the whole family was reunited for a meal. It was unbelievable! It seemed like a dream. I was congratulated for my perseverance in praying to St. Joseph and one of the parties involved, whose faith had unfortunately grown weak, was not afraid to proclaim loudly that this was indeed a miracle. Since then, there is no longer any dissension among us; instead our hearts are joined in loving union.

"Praise and blessings to our good St. Joseph!"

✠

Prayer for Our Family

Great St. Joseph, thou wert chosen by God to be the Head of the Holy Family. Kindly look down upon us and bestow thy fatherly protection upon our home.

Model of the most lively faith, obtain for all the members of our family the grace to believe firmly what God has revealed and to bear witness to our faith in all that we do.

May we ever remain bound together by the ties of true Christian love in the unity of the Holy Catholic Church and taste the peace that Jesus has promised His true disciples.

Grant that we may all love one another as children of God and work together for the salvation of souls, in order to fulfill our role in the great family of the Church and be reunited after this life in the happiness of Heaven. Amen.

In honor of St. Joseph

Do all in our power to establish peace and stability in families by practicing the necessary virtues of charity, obedience, patience, meekness and forgiveness.

TWENTY-SEVENTH DAY

Good and Faithful Servant

It is a general rule for all extraordinary graces granted to a rational being that whenever the divine goodness chooses to raise someone to a special grace or a sublime state, it bestows on the chosen person the charisms necessary for his mission, thus considerably augmenting his prestige.

This principle was especially borne out in the great St. Joseph, putative father of Our Lord Jesus Christ and true husband of the Queen of the World and Sovereign of Angels. Chosen by the Eternal Father as faithful foster-father and guardian of His most precious treasures, his spouse and the Son of God, he has carried out that task most faithfully. Therefore, the Lord says to him: *Good and faithful servant, enter into the joy of thy Lord.*[1]

If we compare St. Joseph to the whole Church, is he not that chosen, privileged man, with whose collaboration, and under whose mantle, Christ was

1. *Mt* 25:21, 23.

brought into the world with propriety and honor? If, then, the whole Church is indebted to the Virgin Mother, since it is through Mary that she has been rendered worthy to receive Christ, without any doubt, after the Virgin, it is to Joseph that the Church owes singular gratitude and devotion. It is he, in fact, who is the key to the Old Testament, by means of whom the dignity of the patriarchs and the prophets has garnered the fruit of the promise. Moreover, he alone has tangible possession of what the divine condescension promised them.

He is, therefore, rightly prefigured by that patriarch Joseph who stored wheat for the peoples.[2] But he also surpasses him, because not only has he provided the bread of material life for the Egyptians, but it is for all the elect that he has nourished with very great solicitude the Bread of Heaven which imparts Heavenly life.[3]

Certainly the intimacy, respect and high dignity with which Christ surrounded him during his earthly life, as a Son towards His father, cannot be doubted. He did not withdraw these in Heaven, but rather perfected them and carried them to the highest degree. It is, therefore, with good reason that the Lord adds to the saying quoted above: *Enter into the joy of thy Lord.* Moreover, although it is rather the joy of eternal happiness which enters a man's heart, the Lord, nevertheless, prefers to say to him: *Enter into the joy.* In that way, He willed to

2. Cf. *Gn* 41:47-56.
3. Cf. *Jn* 6:50-52.

indicate mysteriously that this joy is not only in him, but that it encompasses him on all sides, absorbs him, engulfs him like a bottomless abyss.

Remember us, therefore, Blessed Joseph, intercede for us by the suffrages of your prayer to Him who was considered your Son; at the same time, obtain for us the favor of the Blessed Virgin, your Spouse and the Queen of Heaven where the Father and the Son and the Holy Spirit reign world without end (St. Bernardine of Siena).

Prodigal Parents and Prodigal Son

A family from Lyons had a son who seemed destined to be their crown in the eyes of men and in the eyes of God. This pious young man felt himself called to leave the world and to consecrate himself to the Lord in the religious life. Hurt by this resolve, his parents fell into his arms, shedding so many tears and reproaching him so much that they succeeded in shaking his resolution; they secured at least a delay.

They then pushed him into the world in order to change his inclinations, and the young man too easily let himself fall into the trap. Very soon he neglected his religious observances, withdrew from the sacraments and surrendered to all kinds of licentiousness.

To escape from the shame of his scandals and from the reproofs of his parents, he left the country and enlisted in the army. His father and mother were grieved, overcome with remorse and sorrow; they scarcely dared to speak anymore to God after stealing from him their child to hand him over to the devil. The thought occurred to them of addressing themselves to St. Joseph in order to obtain at one and the same time their pardon and the conversion of their son. They began, therefore, a novena along with several pious persons and prayed most fervently.

They had hardly prayed a few days when the prodigal son knocked at the door of his father's house and threw himself in tears at the feet of his parents. He was completely changed. The father and mother burst out into tears and embraced in forgiveness this ungrateful son who had become a Christian again. With him joy entered again under their roof. They owed it to St. Joseph, and they rendered him solemn acts of thanksgiving.

Let us learn from this example how important it is to listen to the voice of God and to answer the gift of our vocation. Let us speak to St. Joseph, for he will give us the strength to conquer all the loathing of nature.

✠

Liturgical Prayer

(Postcommunion from the Mass of St. Joseph, March 19th)

Be present with us, merciful God, and through the prayers of the blessed confessor Joseph on our behalf, keep safe the gifts with which Thy goodness surrounds us. Through Our Lord Jesus Christ, Thy Son, who liveth and reigneth with Thee in the unity of the Holy Spirit, One God, world without end. Amen.

In honor of St. Joseph

Obtain from him a greater love for the Church, entrusting all her needs to him, that she may faithfully accomplish her task of evangelization for the salvation of souls.

TWENTY-EIGHTH DAY

The Death of St. Joseph

One day before he died, being wholly inflamed with divine love on account of these blessings, St. Joseph was wrapped in an ecstasy which lasted twenty-four hours. The Lord Himself supplied strength for this miraculous intercourse. In this ecstasy, the Blessed Trinity commissioned and assigned him as the messenger of our Saviour to the holy Patriarchs and Prophets of Limbo; and commanded him to prepare them for their issuing forth from this bosom of Abraham to eternal rest and happiness.

When St. Joseph issued from this ecstasy, his face shone with wonderful splendor. He asked his Blessed Spouse to give him her blessing; but she requested her Divine Son to bless him in her stead, which He did. Then the great Queen of humility, falling on her knees, besought St. Joseph to bless her, as being her husband and head. Not without divine impulse the man of God fulfilled this request for the consolation of his most prudent Spouse. She kissed the hand with which he blessed her and asked him to salute the just ones of Limbo in her name. The most humble Joseph, sealing his life with an act of self-abasement, begged her to grant him her assistance and intercession in this hour of his passing away. The holy man also rendered humblest thanks to her Son for all the blessings of his life and especially for those received during this sickness. The last words which St. Joseph spoke to his Spouse were:

"Blessed art Thou among all women and elect of all the creatures. Let angels and men praise Thee; let all the generations know, praise and exalt thy dignity; and may in Thee be known, adored and exalted the name of the Most High through all the coming ages; may He be eternally praised for having created Thee so pleasing in His eyes and in the sight of all the blessed spirits. I hope to enjoy thy sight in the heavenly fatherland."

Then this man of God, turning toward Christ Our Lord, in profoundest reverence, wished to kneel before Him. But the sweetest Jesus, coming near, received him in His arms, where, reclining his head upon them, Joseph said:

"My highest Lord and God, Son of the Eternal Father, Creator and Redeemer of the World, give Thy blessing to Thy servant and the work of Thy hand. I extol and magnify Thee and render eternal and heartfelt thanks to Thee for having, in Thy ineffable condescension, chosen me to be the Spouse of Thy true Mother; let Thy greatness and glory be my thanksgiving for all eternity."

The Redeemer of the world gave him His blessing, saying:

"My father, rest in peace and in the grace of My Eternal Father and Mine; and to the prophets and saints, who await thee in limbo, bring the joyful news of the approach of their redemption."

At these words of Jesus, and reclining in His arms, the most fortunate St. Joseph expired, and the Lord Himself closed his eyes. At the same time the multitude of angels, who attended upon their King and Queen, intoned hymns of praise in loud and harmonious voices. By command of the Lord they carried his most holy soul to the gathering-place of the Patriarchs and Prophets, where it was immediately recognized by all as clothed in the splendors of incomparable grace, as the putative father and the intimate friend of the Redeemer, worthy of highest veneration. Conformably to the will and mandate of the Lord, his arrival spread unutterable joy in this countless gathering of the saints by the announcement of their speedy rescue (Venerable Mary of Agreda).

The Happy Death of an Irishman in South Africa

An Irish missionary Bishop was, for several years, given charge of an area as large as England in South Africa.

From time to time, he would visit his widely dispersed flock. On one of these trips he got lost.

Not knowing what to do, he invoked his guardian angel, St. Joseph and Our Lady of Good Counsel and then continued his journey, completely disoriented. Finally, he arrived at a group of houses. A peasant-farmer happened to be working near his house. "You have come at an opportune time," he said to his visitor. "A man is dying next door."

The Bishop went in to the dying man. Upon seeing him, the latter began to weep with joy and cried out: "O, St. Joseph! I knew that you would send me a priest before I died."

"How so?" the missionary asked him.

The sick man then told him: "I am Irish and when I was a child my mother taught me to pray to St. Joseph: 'O St. Joseph, obtain for me the grace of a holy death.' I have said this prayer every day of my life. At the age of 21, after having fought in the war against the Kaffirs, I stayed here in Africa. I fell ill and I prayed to St. Joseph with even more fervor, and now he has sent me a priest in this most unexpected way."

The following day, the sick man died in peace.

The Poor Souls and St. Joseph

A young girl, brought up in a house of the Sacred Heart, was chosen by God for a great work. From her tenderest years she often asked herself this question: "God is our Providence, how can we become His?" And grace put this answer into her heart: "By paying the debt of Purgatory."

On November 2, 1853, a plan was laid to establish a religious congregation, whose chief aim would be to come to the aid of these poor souls by work, prayer and suffering. The saintly Curé of Ars, delighted with the idea, gave it his entire support, often sending counsel and advice to the holy foundress who would become Blessed Mary of Providence.

A promise was made to St. Joseph that, if the work took shape, the first statue to be placed in the mother-house of those consecrating themselves entirely to the relief of the souls in Purgatory, would be his. St. Joseph took good care not to forget this promise. Providence brought about the acquisition of a residence in Paris, and the Sisters took the name of Helpers of the Souls in Purgatory (Auxiliatrices des Ames du Purgatoire). As early as the following day, a postman arrived and delivered a statue of the saint, sent by a person who knew nothing of either the pious intention or even the acquisition. Thus St. Joseph was pleased to declare himself the protector of this heroic work, pursuing a hidden ministry in the heart of the great city of Paris.

✠

Prayer for the Dying

Eternal Father, by Thy love for St. Joseph, whom Thou didst select from among all men to represent Thee upon earth, have mercy on us and on the dying.

Our Father, Hail Mary, Glory be.

Eternal Divine Son, by Thy love for St. Joseph, who was Thy faithful guardian upon earth, have mercy on us and on the dying.

Our Father, Hail Mary, Glory be.

Eternal Divine Spirit, by Thy love for St. Joseph, Who so carefully watched over Mary, Thy beloved Spouse, have mercy on us and on the dying.

Our Father, Hail Mary, Glory be.[1]

In honor of St. Joseph

Commend to St. Joseph the dying who will appear before God's tribunal today; make sacrifices for the conversion of sinners and for the relief of the poor souls in Purgatory.

1. Cf. also Prayer for a Happy Death on Third Day, p. 38.

TWENTY-NINTH DAY

The Resurrection of St. Joseph

Has St. Joseph been raised from the dead? Is he body and soul in Heaven? Let us seek the answer to this question, relevant in the highest degree to St. Joseph's glory and our own devotion to him, in the delightful discourse which St. Francis de Sales, doctor of devotion, consecrated to St. Joseph's virtues:

"What more is left for us to say, except that we must never doubt that this glorious saint wields great influence in Heaven with Him who favored him to the point of raising him there body and soul? All the more probable seems this elevation inasmuch as we possess no relic of him here below on earth, and it seems to me that no one could doubt this truth. For how could He have refused this grace to St. Joseph, to whom He had been so obedient during his lifetime?

"Doubtless on His descent to Limbo, Our Lord was hailed thus by St. Joseph: 'My Lord, recall, if You please, that when You came to earth from

Heaven, I received You into my house and into my family. Receive me into Yours now that You are going there. I carried You in my arms, so now take me in Yours; and as I undertook to feed and guide You in the course of Your mortal life, take care of me and lead me to life immortal.' "

If it is true that by virtue of the Most Blessed Sacrament the bodies of the elect will rise gloriously on Judgment Day,[1] how could we doubt that Our Lord raised to Heaven, at the same time as Himself, in soul and body, the glorious St. Joseph, who had had the honor and the grace of carrying Him so often in his blessed arms, where Our Lord took such delight? O! How many tender kisses did He not bestow on him to reward him for his labor!

If we trust him, he will obtain for us a holy increase in all kinds of virtue, but especially in the most holy virtue of purity of mind and body, the most lovable virtues of humility, constancy, courage and perseverance; virtues which render us victorious over our enemies in this life, and lead us to merit the grace of enjoying, in eternal life, the rewards prepared for those who will imitate the example he gave them while in this life—a reward which will be nothing less than eternal happiness, in which we shall enjoy the clear vision of the Father, the Son and the Holy Spirit. Blessed be God!

---

1. Cf. *Jn* 6:55.

The Gospel tells us that at the moment of Our Lord's death and resurrection, the tombs were opened and many saints rose from the dead.[2] How could Jesus, on choosing an escort from those who had been raised from death to assert even more His own resurrection and to add greater splendor to His triumph, not include His foster-father St. Joseph as first among them? St. Joseph held every possible title to such a favor, titles similar to those which earned Mary her glorious Assumption.

St. Joseph's eminent virginity, which is at the root of his most pure union with Mary, the Mother of God, calls for more than a simple privilege of incorruption for his body, but rather a renewal of life prior to the time appointed for the general resurrection. His standing as Spouse of Mary requires that he be associated, in a resurrected state, with the resurrected Mary. His standing as foster-father and provider for Jesus, postulates his total glorification at Jesus' side. The intimate unity of the Holy Family demands that Joseph as head be in full harmony of glory with the two other members comprising it, Mary and Jesus. It is untenable that only Joseph's soul should be in Heaven, that even the temporary absence of his body should inject an incongruous note into the triumphant aspect of the Holy Family.

Let us repeat with St. Francis de Sales: "St. Joseph is therefore, without doubt, in Heaven, body and soul."

---

2. Cf. *Mt* 27:53.

Let us note that the efficacy of St. Joseph's intercession is bound up with his pre-accomplished resurrection. In Heaven, Jesus offers His Father His sacred wounds and thereby draws down infinite mercies on the world; Mary presents to her Son the womb which conceived Him and brought Him into the world, and this causes an unceasing and repeated flow of graces to descend on souls; in the same way, Joseph raises towards Jesus the arms which carried and fed Him and thus procures countless favors for his faithful disciples. Bodily gesture is not superfluous in the intercession of a mediator (Dom Bernard Maréchaux).

The Gentleman Who Saved an Arab Girl

St. Joseph manifests his kindness everywhere. A little Arab girl who had lost her parents had grown up like a wild plant, without finding any affection. The persons who had given her shelter made her work without giving her much food. She was often beaten, which resulted in making her more unbearable. She ran away several times, but was caught and brought back. The day came when, not being able to take any more, she decided to throw herself into a well in the countryside.

She threw her sandals into the water, so as to leave no trace. As she was about to jump in, she heard footsteps behind her. She turned and saw a man, who said to her, "Anything but that!" He gave her sandals back to her, saying, "Go. I will help you"; then he disappeared. The girl left, wandering aimlessly. On the outskirts of a town she was greeted by a group of girls who were working in a camp. They gave her something to eat, for she was starving.

In visiting the house, the young girl stopped, deeply moved, before a statue, saying, "That's the gentleman who said, 'Go, I will help you.' " It was a statue of St. Joseph, and the house was that of the Good Shepherd of E.B. The girl wanted to know who this gentleman was whom she had seen and had now rediscovered. After St. Joseph, and with him, she discovered the Blessed Virgin Mary, then Jesus Christ and the Church. First came her Baptism, then the religious vocation, then taking the habit, with the name of Sister Madeleine of St. Joseph. After long years of a happy life in the true faith, she went to meet her glorious Protector.

No Diesel Needed

Thanks to the kindness of benefactors who take turns lending them their trucks, the Little Sisters of the Poor in Amiens are able to make very successful begging tours in the countryside.

One Wednesday—the day dedicated to St. Joseph—they warned the Sister Superior that, because of the length of their trip, they probably would not be back before six in the evening. Even so, they were back by noon. Their truck had been filled by the time they reached the second farm.

They unloaded as quickly as they could and set off again to visit the other farms, where they were expected to arrive.

"That's all very well," said the driver, "but my boss wasn't expecting two trips, and I haven't got enough diesel."

"Never mind," said the Sister, "I'll get you a jerrican; just check the tank, and tell me how much you need."

The driver put his dipstick into the fuel-tank and was flabbergasted: it was as full as when he had set off, despite the fact they had already covered some sixty miles (a hundred kilometers).

He was so struck by this that he refused to take the jerrican of reserve fuel which they offered him just in case. And in point of fact, there was enough in the tank for the second trip as well.

Thanks be to St. Joseph!

✢

Act of Consecration and Choice of St. Joseph as a Patron

O Blessed Joseph, faithful guardian of my Redeemer, Jesus Christ, protector of thy chaste Spouse, the Virgin Mother of God, I choose thee this day to be my special patron and advocate, and I firmly resolve to honor thee all the days of my life. Therefore, I humbly beseech thee to receive me as thy client, to instruct me in every doubt, to comfort me in every affliction, to obtain for me and for all the knowledge and love of the Heart of Jesus, and finally to defend and protect me at the hour of death. Amen.

In honor of St. Joseph

Place all our trust in St. Joseph's fatherly care, in matters both spiritual and temporal, in the sufferings of the Church and the sorrows of the world, for our life here below and our journey to eternity. Ask him to obtain for us the virtues needed in our state of life.

THIRTIETH DAY

St. Joseph, Patron of the Universal Church

The Church is a reproduction of Mary; it is the mystical body of Jesus Christ;[1] it is an expansion in space and time of the house at Nazareth. It was in harmony with all His works that God should have placed the Church under the protection of St. Joseph, into whose hands He had placed Mary and Jesus and whom He had made the head of the Holy Family. St. Ambrose sheds dazzling light on this. That great Doctor of the Church calls Mary "the type of the Church,"[2] and in St. Joseph, Spouse of the Blessed Virgin and guardian of her virginity, he sees the type of the episcopate, which is like him in being temporarily the spouse of the Church and guardian of her precious virginity.

He sets up this parallel: on a higher level are Mary and Joseph, and on a lower, dependent level

1. Cf. Encyclical *Mystici Corporis* of Pope Pius XII, 1943.
2. St. Ambrose, *In Lucam*, B. 2, § 7.

are the Church and the episcopate. Joseph especially represents the episcopate and the Pope, who sums up all that the episcopate is. In the same way that the Church is under the sway of Mary, who is her type, says St. Ambrose, so the episcopate and the Pope, who expresses its unity, are under St. Joseph's influence. The Pope and the bishops, in their concern for the Church and the Churches, should find their inspiration in the tender respect and devotion which this great saint showed towards Mary, his virgin spouse. Could there be a more beautiful model?

If we try to understand how this glorious patronage is exercised, we would say that St. Joseph guards the Church with jealous care from the harmful influences of the world in which she lives, but to which she does not belong;[3] he defends her against the attacks of demons and wicked men who are their agents;[4] he supplies her with exterior, and even more, with interior help, procuring for her the most precious outpourings of God's grace, keeping her in peace and tranquillity, despite the furious assaults constantly launched against her. Last of all, St. Joseph expands the Church.

Have you thought about St. Joseph carrying the Child Jesus into Egypt? About this, St. Leo says that "this nation which was abandoned to ancient superstitions was marked by a secret grace for the

3. Cf. *Jn* 17:11, 14-18.
4. Cf. *Eph* 6:12.

salvation which was at hand."[5] Joseph, bringing Jesus into Egypt, sowed there a seed of grace which in its own time would bear fruit in astonishing fashion. See how he expands the Church, he who, as we have said, represents the episcopate, spouse of the Church, and collaborates secretly but powerfully with the labors of the missionaries who broaden her confines. It is through him that Jesus Christ penetrates into areas still closed off by the devil.

Let us honor St. Joseph with our whole soul; with all the joy of our hearts let us honor him with the greatest veneration it is possible to offer a saint, for that is the clear wish of the Church. Let us go to Joseph in our necessities, in our wants, in our worries and in our alarms. His patronage answers to all; he is the dispenser of Divine Providence.

We must beware of going to him only under the pressure of physical need; instead we should seek the growth of our interior life and the deepening of its roots in God. St. Joseph is the patron *par excellence* of the spiritual life, because in his soul the balanced interplay of its powers is in perfect harmony, and his soul is the most adoring, the most prayerful and totally submissive to God's will. Let us go to him to be impregnated with his attitude towards God and his burning love for Mary and Jesus.

Let us go to him to obtain every blessing, especially that of fruitfulness, for all Christian

5. St. Leo, *Sermo 2 De Epiphania*.

families, every religious community and the whole Church (Dom Bernard Maréchaux).

Lo Pa Hong and *Caritas*

In Shanghai in 1934, a lawyer, Lo Pa Hong, fervent Christian and father of nine children, was walking back home. At nightfall he saw a man lying on the ground. Drunk? No! The poor man had collapsed, worn out, abandoned. Lo Pa Hong signalled a coolie to take the poor man to the nearest hospital. There he met with refusal. At this, the coolie put down his charge and disappeared. Then the Good Samaritan himself carried the sick man home on his shoulders, where he could care for him and cure him.

That night Lo Pa Hong could not sleep. One thought obsessed him: "If I could build a hospital with about forty beds, some poor sick people could be saved."

He knew an abandoned cemetery, which was being used for dumping and waste material, and where, at nightfall, heartless women left their babies, who, during the night, would be torn apart and eaten by dogs. He bought the plot of land. The municipal council was generous enough to give him the stones of a wall in the town. Lo Pa Hong had hardly started the first part of the construction when he had to stop work for lack of money. He had only the equivalent of $25 left. What could he do? He bought a statue of St. Joseph and placed it in the center of the plot of ground. Then he spoke to the great saint: "Dear St. Joseph, if you want a house of charity and mercy to be built here, help me; I have nothing left."

Then he started to beg. Would he find hearts and hands open? Truly, one could say that St. Joseph accompanied him! Lo Pa Hong received so much money that he could finish his first building. Still better, he was able to construct sixteen other large buildings, among which were several hospitals, an orphanage for foundlings, a shelter for fallen women, a center for the blind, another for invalids, a professional school for girls and a school of arts and crafts. Then followed thirty-three churches or chapels for the region. All that became a small town, the work of *Caritas*. In five months, Lo Pa Hong baptized two hundred persons, among whom were some criminals condemned to death, baptized just before execution.

Lo Pa Hong talked, begged, prayed and sacrificed himself until December 30, 1937. He died, age 64, a martyr to charity: two men had been hired to assassinate him.

A saint of our time, St. Joseph permitted him to achieve this unequalled work of charity. There is no greater love than to give one's life for loved ones.[6]

6. Cf. *Jn* 15:13.

Prayer to St. Joseph for the Church

O most powerful Patriarch, St. Joseph, patron of that universal Church which has always invoked thee in anxieties and tribulations; from the lofty seat of thy glory lovingly regard the Catholic world. Let it move thy paternal heart to see the mystical Spouse of Christ and his Vicar weakened by sorrow and persecuted by powerful enemies. We beseech thee, by the most bitter suffering thou didst experience on earth, to wipe away in mercy the tears of the revered Pontiff, to defend him, and to intercede with the Giver of peace and charity, that every hostile power being overcome and every error being destroyed, the whole Church may serve the God of all blessings in perfect liberty. Amen.[7]

In honor of St. Joseph

Pray every day for the Supreme Pontiff and the Holy Church, and beseech St. Joseph to grant her many priestly and religious vocations.

7. Cf. also October Prayer for the Church, p. 239.

THIRTY-FIRST DAY

St. Joseph, Our Confidence

St. Bernardine of Siena used to say: "There is no doubt about it; in Heaven, Jesus Christ not only continues to show St. Joseph every sign of the familiarity and respect which He showed him during His life on earth, as Son to father, but adds to them with fresh honors." Notice these two words: familiarity and respect. The Lord, who on earth honored St. Joseph as a father, will certainly not refuse him anything he asks in Heaven.

At this point we ought to add that St. Joseph had on earth no authority over the humanity of Jesus Christ as a natural father would have, though he did, in a certain sense, have authority over Him as husband of Mary who had authority over Him as His natural Mother. Whoever has the right to a tree, also has the right to the fruit it bears. Consequently, on earth Jesus Christ used to respect Joseph and obey him as His superior, and it follows that St. Joseph's prayers in Heaven are treated as orders by Jesus Christ. This is Gerson's thought:

"When a father prays to his son," he says, "his prayers truly are commands."

Now let us listen to what St. Bernard has to say about St. Joseph's intercessory power on behalf of his supplicants: "There are some saints who have the power of protecting in certain specific circumstances; but St. Joseph has been granted the power to help us in every kind of need, and to defend all who have recourse to him with pious dispositions."

That was how St. Bernard put it; St. Teresa confirms his opinion from her own experience and tells us: "It would seem that God has only granted the other saints power to help us in one kind of necessity; but experience shows that St. Joseph can help in every kind of need."[1]

There is no doubt about it: just as Jesus Christ wanted to be subject to Joseph on earth, so He does everything the saint asks of Him in Heaven. When Egypt was laid waste by the great famine, Pharaoh told his people, *Ite ad Joseph!—Go to Joseph!* So if we are in trouble, let us listen to the word of the Lord and take Pharaoh's advice; let us go to Joseph if we wish to be consoled.

It is quite certain that those who invoke him most frequently and with greater trust will receive more graces. So we should let no day pass without recommending ourselves several times to St. Joseph, who, after Our Lady, is among the saints

1. Cf. First Day, pp. 18-19.

the one who has the greatest influence with God. We should ask favors of him, for he will obtain them all for us, provided they benefit our souls. Above all, I most strongly urge you to ask him for three special graces: forgiveness of sins, love of Jesus Christ and a happy death (St. Alphonsus de Liguori).

Go, then, to Joseph, and do all that he shall say to you;
Go to Joseph, and obey him as Jesus and Mary obeyed him;
Go to Joseph, and speak to him as They spoke to him;
Go to Joseph, and consult him as They consulted him;
Go to Joseph, and honor him as They honored him;
Go to Joseph, and be grateful to him
as They were grateful to him;
Go to Joseph, and love him, as They love him still.

⋆
⋆ ⋆

God has willed that men of every rank and condition should have something in common with St. Joseph, so that they should all place special trust in him and have recourse to him as their special intercessor. In the house of Mary and Jesus, other people asked, but Joseph commanded; other saints request, but Joseph orders; and when he gives orders, he gets what he wants.

So it is that Religious of every Order should have a great devotion to St. Joseph and regard him as their founder, because, in the opinion of very many, he was the first to take the holy vows.

Priests, at the head of your Order, you will find St. Joseph, the first administrator of Jesus' inheritance; consequently, you must have a special devotion to him. Lay Christian faithful, you too can count him as one like yourselves; it is true that he lived as a virgin, but he was also married, and did not live in the temple, even though his house was a sanctuary. And you, working men, laborers, the poor and the needy, you should put your trust in St. Joseph, too, for he lived in a workshop just like you and earned his living by the sweat of his brow. Everyone, then, living or dead, should put their hope in St. Joseph, who lived and died with Him who is Life. St. Joseph is the patron of all Christians.

Anyone who is not devoted to St. Joseph is worse than a pagan or a barbarian. So let us resolve to engage in a holy rivalry, and see who can love and honor him most fervently (St. Leonard of Port-Maurice).

"How Does It Feel To Be in the Dark?"

Maria Repetto was born on January 5, 1807, at Voltaggio, to the north of Genoa. At the age of 22, she entered the Order of the Daughters of Our Lady of Refuge in Bisagno. Being of delicate health, she was employed in sewing, then in the infirmary and finally as a door-keeper. As door-keeper, she revealed her great devotion to St. Joseph by advising visitors to have recourse to the Spouse of Mary.

If anyone came to the parlor seeking counsel and help from her, she would ask the visitor to wait a moment while she went and prayed before a statue of St. Joseph in the adjoining corridor. A moment later, she would return and give the awaited reply.

On one occasion, the wife of a man who had become blind asked for the prayers of the Sister. She exhorted the wife to pray to St. Joseph, while she went into her room, turned towards the wall the picture of the holy patriarch and asked him, "How does it feel for you yourself to be in darkness?"

The following day, the woman returned and announced that her husband had recovered his sight. Immediately, Sister Mary ran to her room and turned the picture back, saying, "So you understood what it meant to be in darkness?" Then, with simplicity she added, "Thank you St. Joseph."

A Loving Sister and St. Joseph's Statue

A young merchant seaman left his native village for a voyage from Le Havre to Marseille. As she said good-bye to him, his loving sister placed a little statue of St. Joseph in his pocket and prayed to that great saint to bless his voyage and bring her beloved brother back safe and sound. When the ship was off Cadiz, the pilot ordered the young seaman aloft to adjust one of the sails. Unfortunately, the rigging was rotten, and while he was carrying out his task, the rope snapped and he fell headlong into the sea. For a whole hour he struggled to stay afloat amid the waves and to swim towards his ship, which never seemed to get any nearer. His hands were getting numb and exhaustion setting in, when he remembered the little statue of St. Joseph and his sister's prayers. Immediately, he plucked up courage, and he sent up a fervent and confident prayer to his patron, promising to have a Mass offered if he was saved from his peril.

His prayer was immediately granted, for he could feel himself buoyed up upon the waves by an unseen hand, and eventually he regained the deck of the ship after catching a line thrown to him by one of the sailors.

Saved by the evident protection of St. Joseph, the thankful young sailor hastened to fulfill his vow and attended the Mass of thanksgiving with all his family, praying to the husband of Mary to preserve and deliver him from all future danger.

So, too, we should pray to this great saint to bless our journeys and the course of our lives, and to defend us from every danger.

+

Prayer to St. Joseph for Perseverance

O dear St. Joseph, foster-father of our Divine Redeemer, and Spouse of our holy Mother Mary, thou didst live with them and toil for them through all the years of the hidden life, and thou didst die in their arms. By the love thou bearest to them and the love they bear to thee, pray for us always and guard us. Obtain for us, O patron of a happy death, the grace to live and die in God's love and favor, that we may spend our eternity with Jesus and Mary and with thee, O dear St. Joseph. Amen.

In honor of St. Joseph

Ask God for the grace to persevere in our resolutions and in devotion to St. Joseph; consecrate ourselves to his powerful patronage, together with all our family, friends and interests.

Epilogue

What can I say here about that man hidden with Jesus Christ? Where shall I find a light powerful enough to break through the darkness which surrounds the life of St. Joseph? And what business is it of mine to expose to the light of day what Scripture has veiled in mysterious silence? If it is the will of the Eternal Father that His Son should be hidden from the world, and St. Joseph with Him, then perhaps we should simply adore the secrets of His providential design without trying to fathom them, and so, perhaps, it would be better to leave St. Joseph's hidden life as a subject for our veneration rather than a subject for discussion. Even so, we must consider it, because it is salutary to meditate on such a fine subject. Let me at least say that though Joseph had the honor of spending every day with Jesus Christ, and that with Mary he had the greatest share of Christ's graces, nonetheless, St. Joseph lived a hidden life, with his actions and virtues known to none. May such a fine example teach us that one can be great without being brilliant, happy without trumpeting it abroad, and have real glory without the help of fame, just by the testimony of one's conscience: *Gloria nostra hæc est, testimonium conscientiæ nostræ—For our glory is this, the testimony of our conscience*;[1] bearing this in mind will help us to despise worldly glory.

But if we really want a solid understanding of the greatness and glory of St. Joseph's hidden life, we need to go back to the beginning. The first thing that strikes one is the infinite variety of vocations displayed by Providence. But among all vocations, I would single out in Holy Scripture two contrasting types: those of the Apostles, and that of Joseph. Jesus is revealed both to the Apostles and to Joseph, but in very different contexts. He is revealed to the Apostles so that He may be announced through the whole of creation, while He is revealed to Joseph to be kept silent and hidden. The Apostles are lights to illumine Jesus for the world, while Joseph draws a veil over Him, and this veil hides Mary's virginity and the greatness of the Redeemer of our souls. So we read in Scripture that when they wished to pour scorn on Him, they said, "Is he not Joseph's son?"[2] So much is this so, that Jesus, for the Apostles, is a word to be preached: *Prædicate verbum Evangelii huius—Preach the word of this Gospel*,[3] while for Joseph, Jesus is a hidden word: *Verbum absconditum*,[4] which it is forbidden to reveal. If we follow this up, we see the same story repeated. The Apostles preach the

1. *2 Cor* 1:12.
2. Cf. *Jn* 6:42; *Mt* 13:55.
3. Cf. *Mc* 16:15
4. Cf. *Lc* 18:34.

Gospel to such effect that the sound of their preaching even reaches Heaven, and St. Paul dares to say that the heavenly powers only became aware of the designs of the Divine Wisdom through the intermediary of the Church and the ministry of her preachers.[5] By contrast, Joseph, when he hears wondrous things spoken of Jesus Christ, listens, wonders, and keeps silent.

So we, too, should value and love this hidden life that enwrapped Jesus and Joseph. What does it matter whether other people see us? Not to be content that God alone sees us is surely the madness of ambition, and it is certainly an insult to Him not to be happy to have Him as sole witness. Maybe we are engaged in important work and hold positions of great responsibility, but even if we spend our lives under the spotlight of public attention, at least let us consider earnestly that our death will be a very private affair, since we cannot take our honors with us. We must reflect seriously on the truth of all this and not allow the clamor that surrounds us to drown out the words of the Son of God. He never said, "Happy are they who are praised!" but He does say in the Gospel, "Happy are they who are cursed because of their love for Me!"[6] (Bossuet)

5. Cf. *Ep* 3:10.

6. Cf. *Mt* 5:11; *Lc* 6:22.

APPENDIX I

A Great Servant of St. Joseph: Blessed André of the Oratory of St. Joseph in Montréal, Canada

(Homily of Pope John Paul II on the occasion of the beatification of Brother André, May 23, 1982)

In Blessed Brother André Bessette we venerate a man of prayer and a friend of the poor, a man whose life-style was truly astonishing.

His life work, his long life of ninety-one years was that of a poor and humble servant: *Pauper, servus et humilis*, as is written on his tomb. A manual laborer until the age of twenty-five, on the farm, in the workshop, in the factory, he entered next into the Order of the Brothers of the Holy Cross, who entrusted him, for more than forty years, with the task of porter in their Montréal college. Finally, for more than thirty years, he was guardian of the Oratory of St. Joseph near the college.

Whence his unforgettable glow, his renown among millions of persons? A daily crowd of sick, the afflicted and the poor of all sorts, those who were handicapped or wounded by life, would find in him, in the college parlor or at the Oratory, a welcome, a ready ear, comfort and faith in God, confidence in the intercession of St. Joseph—in short, the way of prayer and the sacraments, and with that, hope and, very often, the clear and evident relief of body and soul. Have not the poor of today as much need of such love, such hope, such an education in prayer?

But what made Brother André capable of this? God was pleased to endow with a charm and marvelous power this simple man who had himself known the misery of being an orphan, along with his twelve brothers and sisters. He had been left without money, without education, with poor health—in short, deprived of everything but great confidence in God. It is not surprising that he felt so close to the life of St. Joseph, the poor exiled worker so close to the Saviour, whom Canada, and especially the Congregation of the Holy Cross, have always highly honored. Brother André had to put up with misunderstanding and ridicule because of the success of his apostolate. However, he remained simple and jovial. By recourse to St. Joseph and before the Blessed Sacrament, he himself recited, in the name of the sick, the long and fervent prayers which he taught them.

Is not his confidence in the virtue of prayer one of the most precious directives for the men and women of our day who are tempted to solve their problems without God?

APPENDIX II

Diverse Prayers in Honor of St. Joseph

Spiritual Communion in Honor of St. Joseph

O Jesus, my Divine Saviour, like a meek and gentle lamb Thou didst offer Thyself upon the cross as a sacrifice for the whole world, and in Thine own Most Precious Blood didst wash away our sins.

On our altars Thou dost renew the sacrifice of the cross, and givest Thyself, moreover, to us as the food of our souls. I may not now receive Thee really in the Blessed Sacrament, but my soul sighs and longs for Thee, and therefore I beseech Thee in Thy love and mercy to unite Thyself to me, at least in a spiritual manner. Thou didst condescend to heal so many, when they but touched the hem of Thy garment. Permit me now, good Master, gentle Saviour, to touch Thee in spirit and with confidence that my poor soul may be freed from all its ills.

Come to me, Jesus, come, and remain with me always; let me nevermore be separated from Thee by sin. I thank Thee for all Thy graces and blessings. I love Thee above all things and with my whole heart. Bless me, that I may persevere in Thy service to the end of my life.

Dear St. Joseph! how great, how innumerable were the graces which thou didst receive, when the Divine Child dwelt under thy roof! How inexpressible was the happiness of thy heart, when thou didst carry Him in thine arms! Pray for me, holy foster-father of Jesus, my Saviour, that this spiritual communion may be most salutary to me, that the strength of the Most Blessed Sacrament may be my support in all the trials and temptations of life, that it may strengthen me in all good, and help me to win the crown of eternal glory. Amen.

Priest's Prayer to St. Joseph before Holy Communion

Happy and blessed art thou, O Blessed Joseph, to whom it was given not only to see and hear that God whom many kings desired to see and saw not, to hear and heard not; but also to hold Him in thine arms, to embrace Him, to clothe Him, to guard and defend Him.

℣. Pray for us, O blessed Joseph.

℟. That we may be made worthy of the promises of Christ.

Let us pray

O God, Who hast given unto us a royal priesthood, vouchsafe, we beseech Thee, that as Blessed Joseph was found worthy to touch with his hands Thine only-begotten Son, born of the Virgin Mary, so we may be made fit, by cleanness of heart and purity of work, to serve at Thy holy altars; that we may worthily receive the Most Sacred Body and Blood of Thy Son, now in this present world, and deserve to attain an everlasting reward in the world to come. Through the same Christ Our Lord. Amen.

Offering of Mass and Communion for Religious on Wednesday in Honor of St. Joseph

O Divine Jesus! Lamb without spot, Whose Precious Blood was shed for the redemption of mankind, I adore Thee in the mystery of faith and love, in which, by Thy exceeding great mercy, Thou dost daily renew the sacrifice of Thyself for man. Deign to destroy in me all that is displeasing to Thy pure eyes, in order that I may be as a living holocaust, pleasing and acceptable before the throne of Thy love.

O Mary, I have recourse to thee in this happy moment; pray for me, that my heart may be penetrated with profound humility, lively faith, and ardent love during the celebration of this august sacrifice.

O glorious St. Joseph, first adorer, after Mary, of the sacred humanity of my Saviour, to thee do I confide my friends and benefactors, and those for whom I have promised to pray, especially. . . . Obtain for them all the graces thou knowest to be necessary for them; take under thy protection all our temporal interests; obtain for our Superiors wisdom and justice in the discharge of their authority, and obtain for me, O holy St. Joseph, a perfect spirit of poverty, chastity, and obedience, and a happy death. Amen.

Liturgical Prayers after Holy Communion in Honor of St. Joseph

We who have been refreshed at the fountain of divine blessing, pray Thee, Lord Our God: that as Thou dost gladden us by the protection of Blessed Joseph, so by his merits and intercession Thou wouldst make us partakers of everlasting glory. Through Our Lord Jesus Christ, Thy Son, who liveth and reigneth with Thee in the unity of the Holy Spirit, One God, world without end. Amen.

May these holy mysteries, which we have received, O Lord, by the intercession of St. Joseph, make up what is wanting in our works and be an assurance of Thy rewards. Through Our Lord Jesus Christ, Thy Son, who liveth and reigneth with Thee in the unity of the Holy Spirit, One God, world without end. Amen.

Lord, Thou dost renew us with these life-giving sacraments: may we always live in holiness and justice. Let our constant help be the prayers and example of Joseph, the just and obedient man, who helped to carry out the great mysteries of our salvation. Through Our Lord Jesus Christ, Thy Son, who liveth and reigneth with Thee in the unity of the Holy Spirit, One God, world without end. Amen.

October Prayer to St. Joseph for Holy Church

(Composed by Pope Leo XIII)

To thee, O blessed Joseph, we have recourse in our affliction, and, having implored the help of thy thrice-holy Spouse, we now, with hearts filled with confidence, earnestly beg thee also to take us under thy protection.

By that charity wherewith thou wert united to the Immaculate Virgin Mother of God, and by that fatherly love with which thou didst cherish the Child Jesus, we beseech thee and we humbly pray that thou wilt look down with gracious eye upon that inheritance which Jesus Christ purchased by His Blood, and wilt succor us in our need by thy power and strength.

Defend, O most watchful guardian of the Holy Family, the chosen offspring of Jesus Christ. Keep from us, O most loving Father, all blight of error and corruption. Aid us from on high, most valiant defender, in this conflict with the powers of darkness; and even as of old thou didst rescue the Child Jesus from the peril to His life, so now defend God's holy Church from the snares of the enemy and from all adversity. Shield us ever under thy patronage, that, following thy example and strengthened by thy help, we may live a holy life, die a happy death, and attain to everlasting bliss in Heaven. Amen.

Prayer of a Religious to the Glorious Patriarch St. Joseph, Foster-father of the Eternal Word, Spouse of the Most Holy Virgin, Model and Patron of Interior Souls

Dear St. Joseph! man according to the Heart of God! Seraph of love! thou, whose heart was always on fire with the pure flames of the most ardent charity, and whose life was a constant prayer and continual contemplation! deign to accept me as thy protégé, and to teach me the perfection of the interior life. Teach me how to model my heart in accordance with the Hearts of Jesus and Mary. Direct me in the way of salvation, and obtain for me that I may, day after day, without interruption, live and labor for God and my neighbor in the rigorous observance of my vows. From the height of thy throne, where thou reignest in Heaven near Jesus and Mary, cast thy paternal and compassionate looks upon all Religious and especially upon those of our own Order, who are filled with the most profound respect and tender veneration for thee. Be a father to us all; inspire our Superiors; protect our interests; shield us from danger and aid us in the spread of God's kingdom on earth. Obtain for all Religious the graces of which they stand in need, in order to arrive at the sanctity to which God calls them. Especially obtain for them the spirit of prayer, the gift of piety, that fervor of which thou art the perfect model. Teach them to pray as thou thyself hast learned it from Jesus and Mary.

May they be always animated with the same sentiments of humility, purity of intention, respect, docility, faith, confidence and love, with which thou thyself wert inflamed and actuated when, in thy hidden life, in the silence and seclusion of thy poor house at Nazareth, thou didst offer unceasingly with Jesus and Mary the most fervent and acceptable prayers to the Divine Majesty. Amen.

Parents' Prayer to St. Joseph

O Glorious St. Joseph, to you God committed the care of His only-begotten Son amid the many dangers of this world. We come to you and ask you to take under your special protection the children God has given us. Through holy Baptism they became children of God and members of His holy Church. We consecrate them to you today, that through this consecration they may become your foster-children. Guard them, guide their steps in life, form their hearts after the Hearts of Jesus and Mary.

St. Joseph, who felt the tribulation and worry of a parent when the Child Jesus was lost, protect our dear children for time and eternity. May you be their father and counselor. Let them, like Jesus, grow in age as well as in wisdom and grace before God and men. Preserve them from the corruption of this world, and give us the grace one day to be united with them in Heaven forever. Amen.

(Courtesy of the Knights of Columbus, USA)

Prayer to St. Joseph to Know One's Vocation in Life

O great St. Joseph, who wert so docile to the guidance of the Holy Spirit, obtain for me the grace to know what state of life Divine Providence destines for me. Do not suffer me to be deceived with regard to so important a choice, upon which depends my happiness in this world, and even my eternal salvation. Do thou obtain for me that, being enlightened to know the Divine Will and faithful in accomplishing it, I may embrace that state of life which God has destined for me, and which will lead me to a happy eternity. Amen.

Triduum for the Gaining of Some Special Grace

1. In the miseries of this vale of tears, to whom shall we have recourse, if not to thee, good St. Joseph, to whom thy beloved spouse Mary entrusted all her rich treasures, that thou mightest keep them to our advantage?

"Go to my spouse, Joseph," Mary seems to say to us, "and he will comfort you; he will deliver you from the misfortunes which now oppress you and will make you happy and contented."

Do thou have pity on us therefore, O Joseph, have pity on us through that love which thou didst cherish towards a spouse so worthy and so amiable.

Our Father, Hail Mary, Glory be.

2. We are fully conscious that we have offended the justice of God by our sins and deserve His most severe chastisements. Now, what shall be our place of refuge? In what haven shall we find ourselves in safety?

"Go to Joseph," Jesus seems to say to us, "Go to Joseph, in whom I was well pleased and whom I had for My foster-father. To him, as to a father, I have communicated all power, that he may use it for your good according to his own desire."

Pity us, therefore, O blessed Joseph, pity us, for the great love thou didst bear toward a Son so admirable and so dear.

Our Father, Hail Mary, Glory be.

3. Unhappily, the sins we have committed call down upon us the heaviest scourges; this we must confess. In what ark shall we take refuge in order to be saved? Where shall we find the blessed rainbow that shall give us comfort and hope in the midst of our affliction?

"Go to Joseph," the Eternal Father seems to say to us, "go to him who took My place on earth with regard to My Son made man. I entrusted to his keeping My Son who is the unfailing source of grace; every grace, therefore, is in his hands."

Pity us, then, dear Joseph, pity us by thy great love for Almighty God who hath been so generous to thee.

Our Father, Hail Mary, Glory be.

Seven Sorrows and Seven Joys Whereby St. Joseph Became More Closely United to Jesus and Mary

1. O chaste Spouse of Mary, most holy, glorious St. Joseph, great was the trouble and anguish of thy heart when thou wert minded to put away privately thine inviolate Spouse; yet, thy joy was unspeakable when the surpassing mystery of the Incarnation was made known to thee by the Angel.

By this thy sorrow and this thy joy we beseech thee to comfort our souls, both now and in the sorrows of our final hour, with the joy of a good life and a holy death after the pattern of thine own in the arms of Jesus and Mary.

Our Father, Hail Mary, Glory be.

2. O most blessed Patriarch, glorious St. Joseph, who wast chosen to be the foster-father of the Word made flesh, thy sorrow at seeing the Child Jesus born in such poverty was suddenly changed into heavenly exultation when thou didst behold the glories of that resplendent night.

By this thy sorrow and this thy joy, we implore thee to obtain for us the grace to pass over from life's pathway to hear the angelic songs of praise, and to rejoice in the shining splendor of celestial glory.

Our Father, Hail Mary, Glory be.

3. O glorious St. Joseph, thou who didst faithfully obey the law of God, thy heart was

pierced at the sight of the Precious Blood that was shed by the Infant Saviour during His Circumcision, but the Name of Jesus gave thee new life and filled thee with quiet joy.

By this thy sorrow and this thy joy, obtain for us the grace to be freed from all sin during life, and to die rejoicing, with the Holy Name of Jesus in our hearts and on our lips.

Our Father, Hail Mary, Glory be.

4. O most faithful Saint, who didst share in the mysteries of our Redemption, glorious St. Joseph, the prophecy of Simeon touching the sufferings of Jesus and Mary caused thee to shudder with mortal dread, but at the same time filled thee with a blessed joy for the salvation and glorious resurrection which, he foretold, would be attained by countless souls.

By this thy sorrow and this thy joy, obtain for us that we may be of the number of those who, through the merits of Jesus and the intercession of Mary the Virgin Mother, are predestined to a glorious resurrection.

Our Father, Hail Mary, Glory be.

5. O most watchful Guardian of the Incarnate Son of God, glorious St. Joseph, what toil was thine in supporting and waiting upon the Son of the Most High God, especially in the flight into Egypt! Yet at the same time, how thou didst rejoice to have near thee always the very God Himself, and to see the idols of the Egyptians fall prostrate to the ground before Him.

By this thy sorrow and this thy joy, obtain for us the grace of keeping ourselves in safety from the infernal tyrant, especially by flight from dangerous occasions; may every idol of earthly affection fall from our hearts; may we be wholly employed in serving Jesus and Mary, and for them alone may we live and happily die.

Our Father, Hail Mary, Glory be.

6. O glorious St. Joseph, an Angel on earth, thou didst marvel to see the King of Heaven obedient to thy commands, but thy consolation in bringing Jesus out of the land of Egypt was troubled by thy fear of Archelaus; nevertheless, being assured by the Angel, thou didst dwell in gladness at Nazareth with Jesus and Mary.

By this thy sorrow and this thy joy, obtain for us that our hearts may be delivered from harmful fears, so that we may rejoice in peace of conscience and may live in safety with Jesus and Mary, and, like unto thee, may die in their company.

Our Father, Hail Mary, Glory be.

7. O glorious St. Joseph, pattern of all holiness, when thou didst lose, through no fault of thine, the Child Jesus, thou didst seek Him sorrowing for the space of three days, until with great joy thou didst find Him again in the temple, sitting in the midst of the doctors.

By this thy sorrow and this thy joy, we supplicate thee, with our hearts upon our lips, to keep us from ever having the misfortune to lose Jesus through mortal sin; but if this supreme misfortune should befall us, grant that we may seek Him with unceasing sorrow until we find Him again, ready to show us His great mercy, especially at the hour of death; so that we may pass over to enjoy His presence in Heaven, and there, in company with thee, may we sing the praises of His divine mercy forever.

Our Father, Hail Mary, Glory be.

Novena of Dedication to St. Joseph

(Feast March 19th – Novena begins March 10th and ends March 18th)

O glorious descendant of the King of Juda! Inheritor of the virtues of all the patriarchs! Just and happy St. Joseph, listen to my prayer!

Thou art my glorious protector, and shalt ever be, after Jesus and Mary, the object of my most profound veneration and tender confidence. Thou art the most hidden, though the greatest saint, and art peculiarly the patron of those who serve God with the greatest purity and fervor. In union with all those who have ever been most devoted to thee, I now dedicate myself to thy service, beseeching thee, for the sake of Jesus Christ, who vouchsafed to love and obey thee as a Son, to become a father to me, and to obtain for me the filial respect, confidence, and love of a child toward thee.

O powerful advocate of all Christians! whose intercession, as St. Teresa assures us, has never been found to fail, deign to intercede for me now, and to obtain for me the particular object of this novena (*Specify it*).

Present me, O great Saint, to the Adorable Trinity, with Whom thou hadst so glorious and so intimate a correspondence. Obtain that I may never efface by sin the sacred image according to the likeness of which I was created. Beg for me that my Divine Redeemer may enkindle in my heart, and in all hearts, the fire of His love, and infuse therein the virtues of His adorable infancy, His purity, simplicity, obedience, and humility. Obtain for me likewise a lively devotion to thy Virgin Spouse, and protect me so powerfully in life and death that I may have the happiness of dying as thou didst, in the friendship of my Creator, and under the immediate protection of the Mother of God. Amen.

Novena in Honor of St. Joseph, Guardian of the Word Incarnate

O Glorious St. Joseph, faithful follower of Jesus Christ, to thee do we raise our hearts and hands to implore thy powerful intercession in obtaining from the benign Heart of Jesus all the help and graces necessary for our spiritual and temporal welfare, particularly the grace of a happy death and the special favor we now implore (*mention it*).

O Guardian of the Word Incarnate, we feel animated with confidence that thy prayers on our behalf will be graciously heard before the throne of God.

℣. O Glorious St. Joseph, through the love which thou dost bear to Jesus Christ, and for the glory of His name,
℟. Hear our prayers and obtain our petitions.

Meditative Novena in Honor of St. Joseph

by Fr. Louis Lallement, S.J.

This novena consists in turning to St. Joseph four times a day (it does not matter when or where) and honoring him in the following four points (only one point to be taken for each visit):

1. His Fidelity to Grace.

By this is meant St. Joseph's consciousness of sanctifying grace in his soul, and his desire to increase that sanctifying grace.

It also refers to his cooperation with the actual graces that God sent to him constantly, that is, graces which enlightened his mind and moved his will to do good and to avoid evil.[1]

Think of this for a minute, thank God and ask through St. Joseph to be faithful to grace.

2. His Fidelity to the Interior Life.

The interior life is the life of the soul, the life of grace in the soul, the life of awareness of God and devotion to duty for the honor and glory of God.

It embraces also the practice of virtue which is associated with living the interior life, such as the spirit of prayer, the continual remembrance of the presence of God, resignation to God's will, humility of heart, the spirit of sacrifice and the like.[2]

Think, thank God, and ask.

3. His Love for Our Blessed Lady.

It means thinking about the devotion of St. Joseph to Mary:

– how he was chosen by her as her spouse;

– how he was told by God's messenger of the mystery of her Divine Motherhood.

St. Joseph was the protector of Mary and Head of the Holy Family. He realized better than anyone else her part in the divine plan for our salvation. His natural love for her was increased and strengthened and perfected by his supernatural love and devotion to her.[3]

Think, thank God, and ask.

1. Cf. also the Fourth Day, pp. 39-41.
2. Cf. also the Twentieth Day, pp. 147-150.
3. Cf. also the Fifteenth Day, pp. 115-117.

4. His Love for the Holy Child.

St. Joseph was told that the Christ Child was the Son of God and the Saviour of the world. He was mindful of the duty which was his of protecting and caring for the Infant Saviour.

His faith in Christ was manifested in the many trials and difficulties that St. Joseph experienced.

His love for Jesus was deep, genuine and profound. It was a love that revealed itself, not only in word, but especially in service.[4]

Think, thank God, and ask.

Ejaculations

Jesus, Mary and Joseph, I give you my heart and my soul.

Jesus, Mary and Joseph, assist me in my last agony.

Jesus, Mary and Joseph, may I breathe forth my soul in peace with you.

Grant us, dear Joseph, to run life's pathway in innocent fashion:

May we forever be safe under thy blest patronage.

O St. Joseph, foster-father of Our Lord Jesus Christ and true Spouse of Mary the Virgin, pray for us.

St. Joseph, model and patron of those who love the Sacred Heart of Jesus, pray for us.

Help us, Joseph, in our earthly strife, ever to lead a pure and blameless life.

A blameless life, St. Joseph, may we lead, by thy kind patronage from danger freed. Amen.

4. Cf. also the Eleventh Day, pp. 89-91, the Thirteenth Day, pp. 103-105 & the Fifteenth Day, pp. 115-117.

Index of Prayers

Index of Stories

Other titles available from
Traditions Monastiques:

I Believe in Jesus Christ,
the Son of God

Jesus Christ and His Church

A Garment of Salvation:
The Scapular of Mount Carmel

Achevé d'imprimer en mars 2003
sur les presses de la Nouvelle Imprimerie Laballery
58500 Clamecy
Dépôt légal : mars 2003
Numéro d'impression : 303083

Imprimé en France

Traditions Monastiques
Abbaye Saint-Joseph de Clairval
21150 Flavigny-sur-Ozerain
FRANCE

Tel: (33) 3 80 96 22 31
Fax: (33) 3 80 96 25 29

e-mail : abbaye@clairval.com